The Macat Library
世界思想宝库钥匙丛书

解析汉娜·阿伦特
《人的境况》

AN ANALYSIS OF
HANNAH ARENDT'S
THE HUMAN CONDITION

Sahar Aurore Saeidnia　　Anthony Lang ◎ 著

刘雨桐 ◎ 译

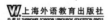 上海外语教育出版社
外教社 SHANGHAI FOREIGN LANGUAGE EDUCATION PRESS

 MACAT

目　录

CONTENTS

引言

要 点

- 汉娜·阿伦特（1906—1975）出生于德国，在第二次世界大战 *（1939—1945）期间移民美国。她的著作对现代政治理论产生了深远影响。

- 她的作品《人的境况》（1958）强调政治行动和多元主义 *（多元主义认为，世界上各种存在形式都应受到尊重）。这两点至今仍是政治学的核心。

- 《人的境况》指出，政治应建立或重塑一种民主参与的政治体制。

汉娜·阿伦特其人

1906 年，汉娜·阿伦特出生于德国，是 20 世纪最具影响力的政治思想家之一。她曾跟随多位著名哲学家学习哲学，如《存在与时间》（1927）的作者马丁·海德格尔 *、《哲学》（1932）的作者卡尔·雅斯贝斯 *。纳粹党执政后，不准犹太人担任任何有意义的职位。因此，身为犹太人的阿伦特于 1933 年被迫离开德国。在巴黎期间，阿伦特致力于帮助那些想移民到巴勒斯坦的犹太难民。在法国难民营被短暂地关押了一段时间后，阿伦特最终与丈夫海因里希·布吕赫 *前往美国。海因里希·布吕赫是一位哲学家，同时也是一位马克思主义 *思想家。马克思主义发展于 19 世纪中后期，是一整套有关政治经济的理论体系，从经济学的角度对社会变革进行阐释，并预言工人革命必将推翻资本主义 *社会及资本主义经济制度。阿伦特与布吕赫大部分时间在纽约工作。

阿伦特发表了诸多涉及革命、政治行动、自由、权力和权威等议题的著作和文章。《人的境况》一书不仅有助于人们了解阿伦特，而且也可作为阿伦特的政治生活思想的理论基石，是其最重要的著作。书中强调政治生活中的行动，而非被动接受。阿伦特认为，真正的政治并非是政府为人民服务，而是公民积极参与到政治中，每个个体要与他人协作，通过不断的革命、抗议活动等行动来重建体制。

　　1951年，阿伦特因出版《极权主义的起源》，首次受到广大读者的关注。在《人的境况》后，她又写了几部有影响力的作品。1961年，《纽约客》杂志派阿伦特前往耶路撒冷，对纳粹官员阿道夫·艾希曼*的审判进行报道。艾希曼因组织运送犹太人到集中营*受到指控，后在以色列接受审判。阿伦特将系列文章集结为书，题为《艾希曼在耶路撒冷》（1963）。书中，阿伦特提出"平庸之恶"，用以形容无脑的官僚们犯下的罪恶。她还指出，纳粹曾利用欧洲的犹太人组织机构"协助"欧洲犹太人走向死亡。这在犹太读者中引起了很大争议。1963年，阿伦特出版《论革命》，将美国革命*（1775—1781）与法国大革命*（1789—1793）进行对比。美国革命以建立美利坚合众国而结束，而法国大革命推翻了王朝，建立起共和国。阿伦特深入剖析了两场革命的差异。此外，她还撰写了与非暴力反抗*（指以和平却违法的行动对政府表示抗议）、暴力、权力、权威相关的文章。在她生命的最后几年，阿伦特转向研究"精神生活"，试图厘清思考、意志和判断三个概念。1975年，69岁的阿伦特逝世，此时她正在进行对最后一个主题"判断"的写作。

《人的境况》的主要内容

　　在《人的境况》中，阿伦特将人类活动区分为劳动、工作和行动。劳动用以满足人类每日的生存需要，如提供食物养活自己。工作是指超越人类生命存在的活动，如科学、艺术及文学。行动是一种特有的政治形式的活动，人类参与到行动中，形成一个共同体。阿伦特认为，"行动"在政治中十分关键，却总是在我们理解"常态政治"时被忽视。尽管很多人将制定经济政策、探讨社会问题视为政治生活的内容，但阿伦特认为，政治的首要问题是关注公民如何积极协作参与建制，反过来这也为公民创造了空间，让他们能够公开地互相显现自我。

现象学＊是一种对主观经验和意识进行结构分析的哲学研究方法（"主观经验"在此仅指属于个体的独特体验）。《人的境况》为使用现象学方法进行政治研究提供了范本。该书重点关注现象，而非探究人类生活或政治的真理。阿伦特将行动视为最关键的人类活动，它不仅事关建制，而且使公民在公共政治空间中互相显现自我。

现代政治往往忽略或误解了"行动"的公共显现，认为行动只在私人生活中显现。阿伦特将私人生活归入社会领域而非政治领域。政治生活中的自我显现意味着通过接受多元化视角下对政治功能的解读，来改善政治观念，重新建制。多元主义指世界上各种存在方式都应受到尊重，人类也将从这些非传统的观念中受益。

《人的境况》对古希腊＊政治经验进行了借鉴，如起源于古希腊雅典城邦的民主制、古希腊哲学家亚里士多德＊的政治思想等。亚里士多德将人类视为会思考的政治演员，而阿伦特强调人类生活中不仅有思想，政治是更重要的一部分。柏拉图＊等古希腊哲学家只将人类视为思想者，这一点在阿伦特看来是错误的。

该书也对马克思主义理论进行了反驳。阿伦特认为马克思主义思想过多关注劳动而忽视了政治行动。她也不认同自由主义*式的政治哲学，因这种政治哲学将政治视为给予个体最大限度的自由，去追求个人利益。阿伦特赞成保护个体的私人空间，但同时也认为民众应通过行动参与到政治中，从而成为真正意义上的合格公民。

《人的境况》介绍并重新定义了一些重要概念。例如，"多元性"（又译"复数性"）的内涵远大于自由多元主义*。"多元性"更加强调为公民提供不同形式的政治参与空间。阿伦特还提出了一个概念——"诞生性"*，即政治应以新制度、新观念的创生为中心。

自始至终，《人的境况》都在提醒我们，我们与这个星球紧密相连，人类的生存不应寄托于来世或"另一个世界"；相反，我们更应关注此时此刻的政治状况，这将为更美好的共同生活创造新的空间与新的制度，从而改善"人的境况"。

《人的境况》的学术价值

在今天，《人的境况》仍具价值。极权主义统治下，中央政府具有绝对的权威，完全控制着人们的私人生活及公共生活，并要求人们的绝对服从。阿伦特生前曾特别关注的极权主义*国家如纳粹德国等，如今已不复存在，但是在21世纪，国家、跨国企业通过监控、技术来统治或控制我们，使我们成为被动的消费者。《人的境况》指出积极参与政治生活的重要性，去反抗不想要的、不喜欢的事情，并创造新的制度。该书强调了政治运动（2010年在中东爆发，总称为"阿拉伯之春"*的民众抗议运动就是一例）的种种益处；尽管有的运动以失败告终，仍可被视为公民持续反抗暴政、创建新体制和构想的"人的境况"的典型事例。

书中对显现世界（即抽象、主观的体验，而非真理）的论述在当今仍具意义。宗教中对来世的关注已渗透进世界许多地区的政治，但在阿伦特看来，我们只与现在生活着的这个星球密切相关；也就是说，人类要齐心协力地面对并解决因人口增多、生存空间拥挤造成的冲突矛盾。我们与其幻想出一个来世的"乌托邦"，不如在今世参与到政治生活中，创建一个公共空间，在其中允许提出不同意见、允许争论，却不会引起暴力冲突。

最后，阿伦特所提倡的多元性、尊重他人的观念，使自由主义不再只是"接纳他人"的老生常谈，而是使自由主义以更加积极的方式对政治产生影响。宽容意味着勉强接受他人的观点，多元主义与宽容不同，它意味着积极对待不同的观点看法，并充分认识他人可以为政治带来益处并对他们表示赞赏。阿伦特的作品告诉了我们"接受多元化观点，而非简单包容差异"的重要性。

第一部分：学术渊源

1 作者生平与历史背景

要点 🔑

- 《人的境况》指出，当人们被限制与世界、与他人建立联系时，政治行动尤为重要。
- 阿伦特在《人的境况》中提出的观点，与她在 20 世纪初受到的德国哲学教育及身为一名纳粹德国犹太人的经历有关。
- 《人的境况》延续了阿伦特对极权主义的思考，并形成了自己的政治观点，即强调"行动"是"人的境况"的决定性因素。

为何要读这部著作？

汉娜·阿伦特的《人的境况》（1958）在出版半个多世纪后仍具价值。虽然政治常会带来冲突矛盾，但阿伦特仍强调生活在地球上的人类的多元性，认为我们会从不同的观点、想法中受益，因此我们要尊重他人，与他人协作，共同创建新制度。不管是宗教原教旨主义＊还是世俗＊原教旨主义（两种信仰体系，寻求向本源或传统的回归）意识形态，均未能承认人的这种多元性，他们认为人只有一种可被塑造至完美的人性。阿伦特告诉我们，尽管我们生活在同一个地球上，但我们并不只有同一种人性，每一代人都应重塑自我。

对阿伦特而言，哲学的普遍原理无法成为政治领域的准则。"偶然性"＊意味着我们无法预测某一行动所带来的后果。阿伦特试图通过关注人类生活中的偶然性、将行动作为政治的核心来改造政治理论。《人的境况》写于第二次世界大战后，当时世界亟待寻找一种新的政治学研究方法，阿伦特的著作在此时给人们带来希望——人类仍是积极的生物，"行动"使我们能够创造新事物。这一观点在当今仍具有意义。这本书是在"提醒我们政治的重要性，提醒我们恰当地理解自己的政治能力，理解政治中暗含的危机与机遇。"[1]

> "在 50 年代早期，汉娜·阿伦特就开始构思一种新政治科学以适应这样一个世界：其中所有的政治事件——世界大战、极权主义、原子弹——都要求哲学家们予以认真的关注。"
> ——伊丽莎白·扬-布鲁尔：《爱这个世界：汉娜·阿伦特传》

作者生平

1906 年，阿伦特出生于德国林登市（今汉诺威市）的一个犹太家庭，其父母无宗教信仰，为社会民主党 * 成员，遵从民主自由，认同财富平均分配的经济政策。1924 年，阿伦特进入马尔堡大学学习哲学，师从德国著名哲学家马丁·海德格尔。学习时对古代历史及古典哲学的关注，影响了阿伦特的思想。1926 年，阿伦特在海德堡大学取得哲学博士学位。她在博士论文中研究早期基督教神学家希波的奥古斯丁 * 的 "爱" 的概念，德国哲学家卡尔·雅斯贝斯任其论文导师。

阿伦特大学期间，德国掀起反犹主义 * 浪潮，某种程度上正是这些对犹太人的敌意和歧视，使阿伦特的犹太人身份在她的学术思想中格外突显，之后她与一些犹太组织及犹太复国主义 * 团体建立了联系。犹太复国主义是犹太人发起的民族主义政治运动，视以色列为犹太人的理想家园。[2]

1933 年，纳粹主义 * 兴起，阿伦特被迫逃往巴黎。在巴黎，她在"抵抗运动" *（以暴力或非暴力的方式反抗德国纳粹统治的组织）工作，为试图逃离欧洲的犹太人提供帮助。1941 年出狱后，阿伦特逃亡美国。在战争快结束时，她曾返回德国并短暂停留，继续帮助犹太难民。之后，她回到美国，成为美国公民，与丈夫海因里希·布吕赫（哲学家、马克思主义者）常年居住在纽约，但阿伦特在全国各大高校任教，并在世界各地演讲。

创作背景

阿伦特在德国的犹太家庭长大，这深刻影响了她对政治、权威、权力的研究兴趣。她的两部早期作品《极权主义的起源》（1952）和《人的境况》（1958），就源于对两次世界大战中发生的骇人听闻的事件的思考。对阿伦特来说，纳粹的极权统治意味着共同的多元文明的终结以及政治的死亡。

阿伦特的犹太人身份对其创作《艾希曼在耶路撒冷》（1963）一书有很大影响。她起初认为以色列是犹太人的理想家园，但后来不再抱有这种幻想，这是因为犹太国家仍在利用纳粹对欧洲犹太人的大屠杀，达到犹太民族主义 * 者的目的。1963 年，一定程度上受到美国政治思想的影响，她写成了《论革命》一书。在其文集《共和的危机》中，阿伦特分析了美国在越南战争 * 中的帝国主义 * 外交政策（即在海外扩大美国文化、经济上的影响力），并指出民众应如何应对。文集中最著名的一篇《论暴力》，探讨了受欧洲列强压迫的殖民地人民去殖民化 *、争取独立的过程。反殖民化运动主要发生在非洲，但中东和亚洲的一些殖民地也在这一时期进行了争取独立的运动。《论暴力》还探讨了美国等国家的学者对在革命中使用武力的辩护。

---

1. 汉娜·阿伦特：《人的境况》，玛格丽特·加诺芬撰写导言，芝加哥：芝加哥大学出版社，1998 年，第 xvi 页。

2. 汉娜·阿伦特的一些关于犹太复国主义及犹太教的著作可参见汉娜·阿伦特：《犹太文选》，杰罗姆·科恩和罗恩·H.费尔德曼编，纽约：兰登书屋，2006 年。

2 学术背景

要点 🔑

- 哲学帮助人们理解现实与存在。

- 沉思哲学 *，一种抽象的、理论化的思考方式，一直被认为是理解现实的最佳途径。

- 阿伦特不认同古典的沉思哲学，而提倡一种更积极、具体的思考方式，这体现在她对自己的身份表述中——她更愿称自己为政治理论家，而非政治哲学家。

著作语境

1958 年，阿伦特发表了《人的境况》。一直以来，自古希腊哲学家柏拉图开始，沉思的传统都主导着西方哲学。沉思哲学关注人的精神生活，重视理论思考多于政治行动，认为思考是一个人参与世界最有价值的活动，并通过寻求超验 * 真理（哲学术语，用以形容超越一切可观察的、可依据经验判断的存在形式）来阐释世界。

阿伦特在世时，学术圈主要分为分析哲学 * 和欧陆哲学 * 两大阵营。为了区分这两类哲学，我们可以说，分析哲学家们主张通过概念化的论证、客观主义 *（认为有独立于精神的实在存在）和逻辑思考现实。他们从科学和数学角度（而非人文角度）分析问题。分析哲学奠基人有出生于奥地利、后入英国籍的哲学家路德维希·维特根斯坦 *、美国哲学家约翰·罗尔斯 *。与之相比，欧陆哲学家的理论更倾向于文学化的表述，而较少有分析性的语言，他们从历史角度进行研究，并且对政治、文化、形而上学 *（抽象事物，如实在的本质、时间等）等议题感兴趣。19 世纪初的德国哲学家黑格尔 * 常被视为欧陆哲学的奠基人。

欧陆哲学的代表人物（均为德国人）还有：19 世纪社会主义思想的创始人卡尔·马克思 *；横跨 19 世纪和 20 世纪的哲学家埃德蒙德·胡塞尔 *、马丁·海德格尔以及尤尔根·哈贝马斯 *。20 世纪开始，分析哲学在英语国家居于主导地位。正如"欧陆哲学"这一名称所指出的那样，欧洲大陆的哲学家大多实践欧陆哲学。但这种地域的划分实则是一种误导，两种哲学主要的不同在其各自的研究方法和研究途径上。

> "《人的境况》质疑了从柏拉图到马克思以来的西方主流哲学传统，这些哲学认为人们已经在理论生活中实现了自己的潜能。对阿伦特来说，这种对理论的强调是对实践的背叛。"
>
> —— 德莫特·莫兰：《现象学导论》

学科概览

20 世纪 50 年代，阿伦特正在进行《人的境况》的写作时，分析哲学与欧陆哲学的论争转向实证主义 * 与现象学的论争。

实证主义重视经验 * 数据（即通过观察得到的信息）和科学方法，排斥形而上学的思辨过程，因此一个实证主义者通过观察和分析事实数据寻找真理。而现象学认为，我们无法用以上这些方法寻求真理，我们面对的只有"现象"，或"表象"。因此我们必须将注意力放在主观经验上，并且最好通过现实本身显现出的样子来认识现实。这种哲学传统并未否认现实的存在，但它认为仅靠实证主义信奉的那种观察和计算的方法，无法真正地揭示真理。

除这两种哲学传统以外，新思潮的出现也对哲学进行了重新划分。20世纪50年代，持续了近半个世纪的冷战 * 开始，世界上的两个超级大国——美国和苏联 * 陷入核武器对峙的僵局，这种对抗对社会科学等诸多领域产生了影响。自由主义传统与马克思理论之间的对抗就深刻影响了学者们定义和回答哲学问题的方式。例如，自由主义传统强调个人自由（涉及经济、社会、政治的方方面面），而在马克思理论中，个人通过既有的共同行动来改变所处的经济体系，进而实现自我。

学术渊源

英国政治理论家玛格丽特·加诺芬 * 曾说，阿伦特"并不关注哲学中的一些主流论辩"，并一直对各种哲学派别表示怀疑。[2] 但在《人的境况》中，阿伦特借鉴了20世纪三位最伟大的德国哲学家海德格尔、胡塞尔以及雅斯贝斯的观点。在强调通过政治行动改造世界的潜力时，阿伦特受海德格尔、胡塞尔现象学的影响，认为我们生活在表象的世界中，因此我们的行动可以从根本上塑造或重塑世界。阿伦特论述了海德格尔在他1927年的代表作《存在与时间》[3]中提出的概念"在世之在"。海德格尔强调人与所处环境之间相互作用的重要性，但阿伦特对此提出批评，认为海德格尔忽视了人类在行为活动中的协作。对她而言，世界存在于人类之间[4]。阿伦特很少将自己视为现象学家，但我们依然可以将她的作品视为这一哲学传统的延续。

在对沉思哲学传统的批判中，阿伦特认同雅斯贝斯的观点，思想渐渐向具体的实践哲学靠近。雅斯贝斯向阿伦特介绍了18世纪德国哲学家伊曼努尔·康德*的政治观点，这使阿伦特用批判的眼光看待古典哲学家。她反对柏拉图的政治哲学，认为柏拉图将哲学凌驾于政治之上；她更赞同亚里士多德积极哲学生活的理念，这与她自己的观点相近。但阿伦特进一步发展了亚里士多德的思想，将政治行动置于最突出的位置；她试图越出沉思哲学传统的藩篱，以全新的方式思考政治。然而这与占主流的美国哲学及欧洲哲学相悖。阿伦特批评这两种主流哲学脱离了人类的行动本身，因此无法真正理解"人的境况"。她的传记作者曾说，"黑格尔派*（指黑格尔的哲学方法，研究思想如何支配现实）哲学家和马克思主义者试图解释历史的全部意义，阿伦特对此表示深深的怀疑。"[5]

这也可以解释为何阿伦特不愿称自己为哲学家，而更愿被称为"政治理论家"或"政治思想家"。[6]

---

1. 参见卡尔·休斯克："1940—1960：人文科学中的新严肃主义"，《代达罗斯》第126卷，1997年第1期，第289—310页；布瑞恩·赖特、米歇尔·卢森编，《牛津大学哲学手册》，牛津：牛津大学出版社，2007年。

2. 玛格丽特·加诺芬：《人的境况》导言，汉娜·阿伦特著，芝加哥：芝加哥大学出版社，1998年，第 xv 页。

3. 马丁·海德格尔：《存在与时间》，纽约：哈珀出版社，1962年。

4. 汉娜·阿伦特：《人的境况》，芝加哥：芝加哥大学出版社，1998年，第52页。

5. 德莫特·莫兰：《现象学导论》，伦敦、纽约：劳特利奇出版社，2000年，第290页。

6. 伊丽莎白·扬-布鲁尔：《爱这个世界：汉娜·阿伦特传》，纽黑文：耶鲁大学出版社，2004年，第327页。

3 主导命题

要点 🔑

- 阿伦特关注"社会性"——认为靠管理者和官员就能解决一切问题的看法——是怎样逐步形成的。

- 政治不应只是一种"家务"式的管理方式,而应创建一个公共领域,使公民得以自由地互相交流沟通。

- 极权主义的兴起是过度政治管理的表现之一,它试图掌控公民的一言一行,而非允许公民按其自由意志行动。

核心问题

在《人的境况》一书中,阿伦特提出的核心问题是:政治行动如何防止极权主义带来的威胁?阿伦特认识到,社会、政治中存在的深层问题为极权政治提供了生根的土壤,我们仍未认识到在创建公共领域以满足公民政治参与时,政治行动的重要作用,而这正是问题的关键。公共领域应当与对经济调控和社会问题的关注分离开来。这一关键问题只关注了社会以及社会需求,却没有正确对待政治问题及由其引发的分歧。因此,阿伦特淡化"社会性"的概念,强化"政治性",她认为与她同时代的遵从抽象、理论的思考方式的沉思政治哲学家们没有认清这样一个事实:对真理、美的反思,在面对极权主义的威胁时,是软弱无力的。

为了与纳粹德国带来的危险相抗衡,政治行动应成为人类生活的基础部分。与德国政治哲学家马克思不同,阿伦特认为,摆脱困境的方法不在于制定新的经济分配制度,或建立新的社会制度,相反地，她认为人们应通过切实的政治实践参与来抵抗新秩序的建立。阿伦特的独创性在于将社会与政治区分开来。她认为，为了防止极权主义统治的兴起，社会要加大对政治领域的关注。

> "社会领域（严格地说，它既非个人的亦非公共的）的出现是一个相当新的现象，它与现代社会同时出现，并在民族国家获得了它的政治形式。在我们眼里，它们（私人领域与公共领域）之间的分界线完全模糊了，因为我们所见的人民组织和政治共同体都是一个家庭的形象，日常事务都由一种巨型的、全国性的家务管理机构照管着。"
>
> —— 汉娜·阿伦特：《人的境况》

参与者

阿伦特关注政治中的管理和控制方式，首先从古典沉思哲学传统的象征——古希腊哲学家柏拉图的著作——中追根溯源。柏拉图认为只有哲学家有资格执政，而阿伦特更倾向于一种参与式政治，并指出"柏拉图式的知行分离仍是一切统治理论的基础"。[1]

一些政治学家、社会学家认为，管理和控制人口是抵抗极权主义的最好方法，但阿伦特不认同这种想法。美国的约翰·加尔布雷斯*、W.W.罗斯托*等自由派经济学家、政治学家认为，政治只应在调控经济时发挥作用；而查理·梅里亚姆*、戴维·伊斯顿*等其他一些当代政治学家认为，自由派的政治管理模式将政治生活简单转化为数据及数字模型。与阿伦特同时代的奥地利哲学家卡尔·波普尔*提出了与阿伦特相似的观点，他在1945年发表的著作《开放社会及其敌人》中指出，从柏拉图到马克思的理论家们都对民主实践表示怀疑，这是因为他们担心民主参与会带来"错误"

的答案。英国哲学家伯纳德·克里克*在极具影响力的《美国政治学》一书中，对当代政治境况提出了另一种观点，批评了以管理学和经济学为主导的政治学。阿伦特也持与他相似的观点。

当时的论战

与同时代的哲学家不同，阿伦特的思想非同寻常。她力求呈现一种新的政治模式，它不依赖于对社会、经济的管理。我们可以将这种模式视为对行为主义*兴起的反馈。当时，行为主义开始在科学、社会学、经济学中崭露头角；正如它的名称，行为主义注重对政治生活中个体行为的分析。但阿伦特注意到，并非所有的行为都是个体行为。尤其是在政治领域，有些行为也会不可预见地在民众的共同愿望中产生，革命及种种抗议活动就属于此类。其他的"行动"以制度、结构的形式存在，这些制度、结构也产生于激进的政治中。行为主义学者更重视数据、管理实践而轻视民主、不同政见及政治生活中的辩论。阿伦特认为行为主义者的研究思路继承了柏拉图政治哲学的研究方法。他们通过允许政府控制人民的日常生活，进而剥夺人民的权利。阿伦特也将论争的目标对准马克思，认为他的政治理论仅仅聚焦在经济因素上。马克思认为，一切政治思想和政治行动都可归因于资本主义经济制度的兴起。虽然马克思主义者与行为主义者的意识形态立场大相径庭，但他们都将经济作为政治的核心。

---

1. 汉娜·阿伦特：《人的境况》，芝加哥：芝加哥大学出版社，1998 年，第 225 页。

4 作者贡献

要点 ⚷

- 阿伦特强调仅存在于政治领域中的行动与行动显现的重要性。

- 阿伦特在《人的境况》中为积极哲学奠定基础，她将积极哲学视为从哲学角度思考政治的途径。

- 阿伦特吸取古希腊民主制度的经验，形成一种以主观经验、意识为认识起点的分析方式，运用现象学的方法阐释政治，从而考察"人的境况"。

作者目标

在《人的境况》一书中，阿伦特致力于考察人类存在及人类活动的境况。一些哲学家认为哲学反思是人类生活中最重要的活动，而阿伦特认为政治行动最为重要，即公民齐心协力，以共同参与、民主的方式建制。她以极具独创性的方式定义"行动"："行动，是唯一不以物或事为中介的，直接在人们之间进行的活动，与之对应的是多元性的人的境况，即不是单个的人，而是生活在地球上的'人们'。尽管人之境况的所有方面都在某种程度上与政治相关，但多元性却是一切政治生活特有的条件——不仅是必要条件*，而且是充分条件*。"[1]

换句话说，多元性是政治生活的起因和动力，人类所能做的最重要的事情就是团结一致，互相尊重，并尝试建立有利于全人类的制度。这些行动从根本上将人类与其他动物区别开来。在阿伦特看来，当代哲学往往忽视了这种作为人类存在的基本条件的多元性。

她将多元性定义为与他人共同生存、尊重他人的观点与行动的情况。

阿伦特在《人的境况》一书中，提供了一种新的政治研究。在抽象观念中，人类被缩限为同一种类型，都有着相同的兴趣和关注点。与此不同，在阿伦特的政治理想中，她接受世界原有的样子，世界上有各种各样的人，他们有不同的兴趣和关注点。对她来说，政治不只意味着治理国家、建设经济、协调社会关系，政治更是同与他人共同生活、共同行动、创造新事物息息相关。

> "1958 年，阿伦特的《人的境况》首次出版，书中对人在公共领域的行动的本质进行了细致的现象学阐释。阿伦特主要借鉴了亚里士多德的思想并借助希腊城邦国家的理想化模型进行思考。"
>
> ——德莫特·莫兰：《现象学导论》

研究方法

阿伦特是首位通过分析两千多年前古希腊民主政治的经验，指出当代极权主义及民主政治存在问题的学者。但她并未简单地将古希腊民主政治范式套用到当代政治中，而是从中获取如何创建新政治形式的灵感。阿伦特通过历史、古代思想反观现代政治，揭示了政治思想的历史延续性。她对当今政治进行细致、批判性的分析，不再进行沉思哲学式的纯粹的理论思考，而是反思政治实践的可能性。在此之前，还没有人用这样的研究方法探究现代民主应是什么样子。

《人的境况》的第一章对"积极生活"*做了综述，将构成积极生活的人类活动分为劳动、工作和行动三类，并阐述了具体的研究方法及研究目标。第二章聚焦于以上三种人类活动发生的场所（公共领域和私人领域）。第三、四、五章依次讨论劳动、工作、行动三种活动。最后，阿伦特运用自己的理论框架对现代世界进行分析，总结为"积极生活与现代"一章。

时代贡献

尽管阿伦特的研究方法颇具独创性，但《人的境况》还是充分借鉴吸收了许多哲学传统与思想。全书的主题——"积极生活"，就直接受哲学家亚里士多德著作《尼各马可伦理学》[2]中"政治生活"与"行动"*概念影响。古典学者、历史学家在研究亚里士多德的政治思想时多将其置于古希腊的社会语境中，而阿伦特将他的思想置于当今世界中，她并未全盘复制亚里士多德的思想，而是借鉴他的思想，使政治理论不再只是探寻真理，而是去寻求一种可行的民主政治范例。阿伦特师从马丁·海德格尔和卡尔·雅斯贝斯，因此深受现象学影响，孕育出她对"在世之在"、人类与世界联系方式的反思。遵循两位导师的研究思路，阿伦特重点关注从历史、存在主义*的维度对人类经验进行描述（存在主义是一种哲学流派，强调宇宙和现实是缺乏秩序的）。对她而言，"人性并不拥有永恒的实在本质，人性仅仅是某个特定的条件。"[3]

阿伦特将"积极生活"置于"沉思生活"之上，以此将自己与海德格尔相区分，并批评海德格尔忽视人类的协作活动[4]，这正是阿伦特思想的独创性所在。海德格尔认为，哲学家应通过反思寻求真理，尽量避免纷乱世界中的现实政治。而在阿伦特看来，正是这样的哲学诉求使海德格尔即使在整个世界陷入战争的苦海时，仍坚持自己的哲学追求。在《人的境况》中阿伦特将政治活动重新确立为人类生活中最重要的活动，并希望提出一种可实践的面向未来的政治模式。她在此基础上进行发展，对人类的三种活动——劳动、工作和行动——进行区分，这正是《人的境况》的主旨所在。

---

1. 汉娜·阿伦特：《人的境况》，芝加哥：芝加哥大学出版社，1998年，第7页。
2. 亚里士多德：《尼各马可伦理学》，马丁·奥斯特瓦尔德译，纽约：麦克米伦出版社，1962年。
3. 德莫特·莫兰：《现象学导论》，伦敦、纽约：劳特利奇出版社，2000年，第306页。
4. 莫兰：《现象学导论》，第288页。

第二部分：学术思想

5 思想主脉

要点 ⚷

- 劳动、工作和行动是人类的三种基本活动，其中"行动"是政治活动的核心。
- 人们与他人协作行动并创造新事物时，政治产生了。
- 阿伦特以古希腊民主政治经验为基础，发展出了自己的观点并更新了政治思想。

核心主题

《人的境况》整本书围绕着"积极生活"（拉丁语 vita activa）的主题展开。阿伦特区分出三种类型的积极生活：劳动、工作和行动。

阿伦特认为，哲学史上并未彻底厘清"积极生活"的以上三个方面。哲学家们不再对三种不同的活动进行区分，而是将其全部纳入一个概念中。阿伦特尝试再次对三种活动进行区分，或许她对政治理论做出的最大贡献就在于对第三种活动——政治行动——的重视。在她所处的时代，就像当今一样，人们总是将政治视为政治家追求个人政治理想和利益舞台，而不是服务公众的渠道。阿伦特希望重塑政治的尊严。

阿伦特对政治行动的关注为政治研究做出了以下三点贡献。首先，她不再从规则、制度的角度考察政治，而是探寻政治参与者的所作所为。在这一点上，她与通过观察人类活动来进行分析的行为主义社会学家有明显差异。行为主义社会学家也希望政治研究从对立法机构等机构的研究中脱离出来，但他们将人类简化为统计学数据，而非真正试图了解人类。

其次，阿伦特对马克思主义及其将经济视为政治基础的观点进行了全面批判。依据马克思主义思想，历史由阶级斗争推动，而经济利益在阶级斗争中扮演重要角色。

最后，阿伦特借鉴古希腊政治模式，提出一种新型现代民主政治。通常现代民主政治寻求一致性和妥协性，而阿伦特强调民主政治中的冲突层面（"争胜"*）。在她的设想中，这些冲突不致引起暴力，反而可以使政治充满生机与论辩，从而创造崭新、高效的政治生活。

> "我打算用积极生活的术语，来命名三种根本性的人类活动：劳动、工作和行动。这三种活动之所以是根本性的，是因为它们每一个都对应着生活在地球上的人类的一种基本条件。"
>
> —— 汉娜·阿伦特：《人的境况》

思想探究

阿伦特认为，"劳动"与人的生命过程相对应，通过提供人类饮食消耗、繁殖的生存必需品，"不仅确保了个体生存，而且保证了物种的延续"。[1] 劳动是持续性的过程，但它无法创造永恒的事物。阿伦特将劳动者比作奴隶，认为既然维持生命的必需品主宰着劳动者的存在，那么劳动者就不是自由的。在这里，所谓的奴隶并非指人被他人所占有，而是指人被生活中的基本物质需求主宰，使我们无法去探寻那些超越当下的日常生理需求的事物。

阿伦特认为，"工作"创造了一个人造世界，其中的半永久物品在自然界中无处可寻。建造者、建筑师、手艺人、画家，提供了这些"人造物品"，[2] 进而形成人类生活的共同世界。工作不同于劳动，因为工作不受自然、生存所限制。人类的活动和创造改造了自然，也催生了举世公认的事物和制度。因此，工作具有某种程度上的自由。但工作作为一种工具，具有目的性，个体以设定好的任务为目标工作，而非依个人意愿自由行事。

"行动"是指摆脱了必然性后保有最大限度自由的活动。它既是手段，也是目的，它在显现的公共空间进行，行动者于其中显现。行动发生在多元性的公共空间中，表现为与他人的互动。例如，我们将街上的游行示威活动视为政治行动，这是因为无论这些抗议示威活动的结果成功与否，它都发生在他人可见的公共领域中，有可见的事情缘由与行动信条。因此，对阿伦特而言，"行动"与"自由"是同义词，都是人类不受规则的束缚创造新事物的表现。

语言表述

阿伦特经常谈到古希腊的政治观念，但并未将其简单套用到当代语境中，而是分两步进行分析，即先对概念进行历史和政治语境下的分析，再对概念在历史进程中的演化及意义进行阐释。

一些读者对《人的境况》中没有系统的论证感到困惑。事实上，要想全面理解阿伦特独特、复杂、非正统的理论思想，读者可能需要反复阅读。作为一个运用现象学分析的理论家，阿伦特在《人的境况》里也遵循了现象学的研究方法，先是通过惯常的含义或其显现出的含义来阐释概念，之后转变概念，呈现其以其他方式或在其他人面前可能显现的表达。她并不急于对某一术语下一个"正确"的定义，而是对显现世界进行考量后对概念进行分类，并在不断运用中完善发展。在《人的境况》第一章，阿伦特举出了此书所有重要的概念，然后在之后的章节里反复提及这些概念。有人指出，阿伦特就像一位印象派画家，她构建了自己的理论框架，提出了核心概念，并对这些概念进行了简单的描绘。[3]

---

1. 汉娜·阿伦特：《人的境况》，芝加哥：芝加哥大学出版社，1998 年，第 8 页。
2. 阿伦特：《人的境况》，第 8 页。
3. 德莫特·莫兰：《现象学导论》，伦敦、纽约：劳特利奇出版社，2000 年，第318 页。

6 思想支脉

- 阿伦特提出了"诞生性"的概念，即通过政治行动创造新事物。
- 在阿伦特的政治行动思想中，她阐释了宽恕是如何改变政治行动的，并赋予宽恕以新的政治内涵。
- 我们有能力通过政治行动创造新现实，这也使我们有能力解决环境问题。

其他思想

《人的境况》中，阿伦特引入了一个概念——"诞生性"。她认为，诞生性使行动可以从无到有地创造事物，就像生育孕育出新生命一样，政治行动创造的事物也是崭新的，如之前从未出现过的新机构、新观念、新空间。当然，就像出生只是生命的起点一样，政治行动也只是叙事中的一部分，其他环节更为重要。但阿伦特指出，政治行动可以全然改变并创造新事物，就像革命可能会带来新的社会政治图景、政治体制可以重塑政治生活一样。

在阐释政治行动中，阿伦特强调的另一观点是宽恕。此前，评论界并未将宽恕看成一个政治概念，但阿伦特认为宽恕在政治生活中占据独特地位，因为宽恕可以使之前的行动、情况与处境得到改变。承诺是一种重要的政治行动方式，可以在人与人之间建立联系。宽恕与之不同，它彻底地切断个体与之前的处境、行动的联系。它通过摧毁已存在事物来创造新事物。宽恕和诞生性都创造新现实，但宽恕只通过推翻既有的行动来实现目标。

> "所有这三种活动和它们相对应的条件都与人类存在的最一般状况密切相关：出生和死亡、诞生性和有死性。"
>
> —— 汉娜·阿伦特:《人的境况》

思想探究

某种程度上，阿伦特提出的"诞生性"仍具有其最初的含义，即诞生是人类存在的起点。但随后，阿伦特发现政治生活与人类出生的相似性，因此为这一概念注入了新内涵，赋予其此前没有的重要意义。诞生性作为政治行动的条件之一，支撑着政治行动的不可预测性：正如我们不知道一个孩子会成为什么样的人一样，我们也无法知道自己的政治行动会带来什么样的结果。

"诞生性"使阿伦特将行动与言说联系起来。她认为，只有通过叙述赋予行动意义，行动才能产生。构建在行动周围的叙事不仅使行动得到显现，也使行动者得到显现。在政治行动中，我们创建新的政治空间，提出新观点，同时也重塑自我。正如阿伦特说的那样："在行动和言说中，人们表明了他们是谁，主动展示出他们独特的个人身份，从而让自己显现在人类世界中，而他们物理身份的显现则不需要任何这类凭借自身独特形体和嗓音的活动。"[1] 对她而言，这意味着当我们叙述自己的行动、讲述我们在公共场所的所作所为时，我们是在创造全新的自我，一次次地创造崭新的现实。

阿伦特从其理论体系中发展的另一概念是宽恕。阿伦特发现，她十分重视的古希腊哲学并未将宽恕视作一种政治美德，而拿撒勒耶稣*认为，宽恕在政治生活中占有重要地位。阿伦特认为，耶稣将宽恕置于极为重要的位置，这使我们改变政治行动，与过去的行动隔绝，同时又创造新事物。"耶稣的宽恕教导中的自由是脱离了报复的自由，它使行动者和遭受者远离报复，否则他们就会陷入一种行动过程的无情的自动循环中，这个循环凭自身永远不会终结。"[2]

被忽视之处

《人的境况》以人与地球的关系开头，也以人与地球的关系结尾。前言里，阿伦特对苏联 1957 年发射第一颗人造卫星伴侣号 * 进入太空的事件进行了思考，卫星发射仅一年后，《人的境况》出版。在阿伦特看来，卫星发射代表着人类第一次将人造物体送入天体运行的空间，这是一个具有重要历史意义的事件。她认为伴侣号的意义不在于发射成功所展示的政治力量，而在于背后隐含的人类对离开地球的渴望。她想知道，这是否是人类试图摆脱并逃离地球限制的第一步。最后，她表达了对人类疏离所生活的世界和疏离赋予人类生命以意义的事物、制度、空间的担忧。人与世界的联系是如何界定"人的境况"的？很少有人对阿伦特的这一思考进行探究。虽然这一论题似乎与环境问题有关，但阿伦特并未集中探讨环境保护问题。通过对诞生性、政治行动的强调，阿伦特清楚地看到，尽管人类有时以一种激进的方式行事，但人类有能力塑造其所生存的世界。阿伦特时刻牢记，我们是怎样受制于特有的境况中，又是怎样受制于人类在地球上的存在的。

---

1. 汉娜·阿伦特：《人的境况》，芝加哥：芝加哥大学出版社，1998 年，第 179 页。
2. 阿伦特：《人的境况》，第 241 页。

7 历史成就

要点 🔑

- 阿伦特的行动理论和政治理论成功挑战了沉思哲学的思维方式，并指出沉思哲学无法真正理解人的境况。

- 阿伦特认为通过协力行动，人类可以创建新世界；在第二次世界大战之后的一段时期，她对行动、政治的这一阐释为世界带来了希望。

- 在《人的境况》发表后几年，许多评论家批评此书表达不清、逻辑混乱。

观点评价

在《人的境况》中，汉娜·阿伦特为重新思考行动与政治做出了重要贡献。她对行动的强调影响了当代政治理论的发展，也对英语世界的政治研究提出了挑战。她认为政治哲学家仍醉心于对柏拉图式真理*（始于古希腊哲学家柏拉图，认为真理可以从理念世界中找寻）的探寻，政治学家过多关注政治体制，而社会学家将一切事物归结于经济力量的展现。阿伦特将政治行动视为人类创造、再创造自我的实践，这使她与一些哲学流派产生分歧，如唯心主义*哲学（认为意识是世界的本原，反对物质至上的哲学传统）、行为主义政治学（强调分析人类行为重要性的社会哲学，通过统计学分析考察人类行为），以及受马克思主义影响的社会学、经济学。此外，阿伦特运用古希腊哲学阐述自己的哲学观点，这也质疑了现代性（广泛应用于历史、哲学、艺术及政治，既指 20 世纪早期的一段历史时期，也指一种研究方法，强调社会政治生活中的技术和科学理性）的内涵。

许多学者认为，现代世界受制于科学技术的进步，这使政治历史研究变得无关紧要。评论界对阿伦特在重新定位政治研究上取得了何种程度的成功仍持争议。她的作品对许多哲学流派提出了质疑，因此很少有人能够欣然接受她的观点。尽管如此，她提出的质疑和挑战在当今的政治研究中仍占一席之地。

> "汉娜·阿伦特是探讨开端的杰出理论家。她所有的书都是讲述不可预料的故事（无论是关于极权主义的奇特恐怖，还是革命的崭新开端），以及对人类开创新事物的能力的思考。1958年，她的《人的境况》一书的出版，为这个世界带来了出乎意料的东西，四十年后，这本书的独创性仍然像当时一样令人瞩目。"
>
> ——玛格丽特·加诺芬：《人的境况》导言

当时的成就

阿伦特将《人的境况》置于历史概念的框架中。她希望提供一种理论框架，以帮助人们更好地理解现代世界以及20世纪以来发生的一系列悲剧事件。她希望自己的政治研究不只局限于学术圈，而是能有更广大的受众。在她所处的时期，世界政治在苏联、美国及其各自同盟国之间的冷战中陷入僵局；阿伦特正是想提供一种当时主流政治语境以外的选择。

美国一些政治学者如约翰·杜威*、路易斯·哈茨*等，提出通过技术变革、实用主义思想来解决政治问题。阿伦特对此表示怀疑，她持一种"争胜"民主（认为民主应以有利于政治生活的冲突为基础建立）的观点，认为政治是在公共领域内采取行动，只给出一些激进的新提议是不够的，还应以新的形式去展现自我。美国实用主义传统认为可以用一切必要的手段解决问题，阿伦特的政治观点显然与此不符。因此，阿伦特得不到冷战双方任何一边的支持。

局限性

虽然《人的境况》在一些领域颇具影响，但其独特的研究方法阻碍了其读者群的扩大。现象学传统关注显现而非某种不可言明的实在，因此将这种研究方法运用到实际政治分析上，困难重重。有人认为阿伦特有关政治行动的思考并无实质性内容。人人都在"行动"，但阿伦特更关心"行动"本身而非行动产生的结果。因此她的思想不适用于寻求具体措施解决实际问题的政治研究。此外，她对马克思的批评使其疏远了许多受马克思哲学影响的哲学家，[1] 连那些与阿伦特有相似的关注点的政治理论家也对她的作品提出批评。例如，美国政治哲学家谢尔顿·沃林*认为，《人的境况》没有从社会维度对民主政治进行充分阐述。[2]

阿伦特没有某一特定的政治倾向。她作为一个移民到美国不久的德国人，在写《人的境况》时才刚刚开始接触美国社会。但她拒绝给自己贴上任何一种政治倾向的标签，认为自己既不属于自由派，也不属于保守派。[3] 也正因其不属于任何政治意识形态，阿伦特政治思想的实际影响力极为有限。

1. 安东尼奥·内格里:《叛乱:构成力量与现代国家》,毛里奇亚·博斯卡利译,米歇尔·哈尔特撰写前言,明尼阿波利斯:明尼苏达大学出版社,2009 年。

2. 谢尔顿·沃林:"汉娜·阿伦特:民主与政治",《杂家》第 60 期,1983 年春夏刊,第 3—19 页。

3.《汉娜·阿伦特:二十年后》,拉里·梅和杰尔姆·科恩编,波士顿:麻省理工学院出版社,1996 年,第 1 页。

8 著作地位

要点 🔑

- 《人的境况》是汉娜·阿伦特的一部关键的理论著作。

- 《人的境况》丰富了阿伦特在《极权主义的起源》中提出的观点；她在之后的《艾希曼在耶路撒冷》《论革命》等主要政治著作中的观点，在此书中也有所涉及。

- 阿伦特未公开发表的政治理论作品也以《人的境况》为理论基础。

定位

1952 年，《人的境况》出版六年前，阿伦特得到古根海姆基金会*提供的赞助，用以研究马克思主义和极权主义。这使阿伦特可以继续思考她在《极权主义的起源》（1951）中提出的观点。《极权主义的起源》是第一部令阿伦特在学界名声大噪的著作。她在书中指出，极权主义产生于殖民主义*（一国对另一被殖民国的不平等统治）和反犹主义（憎恨、歧视犹太人），这两种思想都破坏了人类之间的平等关系。她也指出，民族主义（一种政治意识形态，将爱国视为最重要的政治准则）因其固有的排他性，也有孕育极权主义的可能。

对极权主义的研究，使阿伦特开始探究许多其他议题和问题，以至于她最终也未完成最初的课题。但在过程中，阿伦特发展了许多观点，如对"积极生活"的起源及其产生条件的思考。她在普林斯顿大学、芝加哥大学进行系列演讲时，就发表了这些观点。演讲中区分了劳动、工作和行动三种人类活动，这构成了《人的境况》的理论基础。其之后的著作也对此进行了深入探讨。

阿伦特的著作促进了对政治生活的本质的讨论。"在 1958 年到 1962 年的四年间，汉娜·阿伦特出版了三本书：《人的境况》《过去与未来之间》和《论革命》，所有这些都源于最初的论马克思主义的著作。"[1] 在文集《过去与未来之间》（1961）里，阿伦特从权威、自由、教育、历史等方面对政治行动进行论述，并详细阐释了《人的境况》中提出的理论框架，使观点更加具体清晰。《论革命》（1963）一书中，进一步发展了关于政治行动的典型范例——革命政治——的观点。

> "我着手做了一点关于马克思的研究，但是，一旦领会了马克思的思想，立即就感觉到如果不重新审视整个政治哲学传统就无法研究他。"
>
> —— 汉娜·阿伦特，引自伊丽莎白·扬-布鲁尔：
> 《爱这个世界：汉娜·阿伦特传》

整合

从阿伦特的作品中，我们可以看出她试图建立一种新的政治理论的志向。1972 年她给友人写信说，"我们在我们的生活中都只有一个真正的想法，我们之后做的一切事情都是这一主题的扩展或变化。"[2]《人的境况》是阿伦特学术生涯中极其关键的一部著作，她运用现象学的研究方法，提出了诸多核心观点。她在进一步分析探索美国政治的具体表征后，完善了自己的理论体系。同时，对德国、以色列政治的关注也贯穿了她整个学术生涯。

阿伦特通过寻求一种积极的政治生活，来实现她的政治实践，两件极具争议的事例可对此加以印证。她曾为《纽约客》杂志撰写了阿道夫·艾希曼的庭审报道。艾希曼曾是纳粹官员，1960 年在阿根廷被以色列特别行动小组绑架。对艾希曼的审判是第一次以第二次世界大战中反人类罪进行控告的审判，这场庭审没有在德国而是在以色列进行，引起了国际社会的广泛关注。1962 年，艾希曼罪名成立，被执行死刑。阿伦特参与了审判的全程，她撰写的报告先是发表在杂志上，后以《艾希曼在耶路撒冷》为书名出版。

《艾希曼在耶路撒冷》备受争议，主要有以下两个原因。首先，阿伦特指出，欧洲许多国家的犹太机构曾协助将犹太人运往集中营，因此这些犹太机构也是犯罪同谋。世界各地的犹太群体认为这是阿伦特在指责受害者，但实质上，她是对政治生活中官僚主义的本质提出批评，这在她评述艾希曼罪行时提出"平庸之恶"的概念中得到清晰展现。有人认为这种阐述减轻了艾希曼的罪责，但阿伦特是想指出，"恶"不总发生在宏大叙事、公共领域中；相反，有时"恶"也会隐秘地出现，藏匿于庸常的官僚会议中。这一观点与她在《人的境况》中的观点相吻合，即将政治行动作为个体显现自我的方式，并批评躲藏在官僚体系幌子背后的现代政治。

阿伦特对美国废除种族隔离的讨论，也引起了争议。根据种族间的界限而实行隔离的制度会降低一些个体的地位，或使他们处于被隔离的状态中。废除种族隔离制度试图结束美国黑人群体与白人的隔离状态。1957 年，九名黑人学生想转学到阿肯色州小石城的中央中学。但是阿肯色州州长阻止黑人学生入学，在联邦政府的干预下，九名黑人学生才得以走入校园。反对废除种族隔离制度的白人对九名未成年黑人学生施暴的照片，促使阿伦特 1959 年为《评论》杂志撰写文章，批评黑人学生的父母默许自己的孩子遭受如此不公正的待遇。许多读了这篇文章的人认为这是阿伦特对种族隔离制度的辩解，但她的讨论基于在《人的境况》中对公共、私人领域的划分上，她认为若是没有优先保障儿童和教育的私人领域，则我们也没有可进行政治探讨的公共领域。在她看来，小石城事件使公共领域与私人领域的界限变得模糊。

意义

《人的境况》可以说是阿伦特最重要的作品。它在学界内外都产生了极大影响，也令她获得了国际认可。正如她的传记作者伊丽莎白·扬—布鲁尔 * 所说："在后来的 24 年里，随着大量论文和著作的发表，从《人的境况》到《心灵生活》，阿伦特获得了国际性的声誉，并在当代理论家中占有不可或缺的重要地位。"[3] 此外，《人的境况》对于我们观察阿伦特思想的发展历程来说非常重要。该书提供了一种新颖的政治哲学分析方式，阿伦特的学术生涯十分广阔，我们也应当以更开阔的视角看待这部作品。

《人的境况》关注理论、哲学，这使阿伦特的声誉局限在学术界。《极权主义的起源》（1951）和《艾希曼在耶路撒冷》（1963）为她赢得了更多赞誉，或许是因为这两本书与当今世界发生的事件有更直接的关联。虽然《人的境况》不是阿伦特最受欢迎的作品，但它可能是阿伦特最重要的理论著作；要真正读懂她的其他作品，我们首先要理解《人的境况》中相关的理论阐释。

1. 伊丽莎白·扬－布鲁尔：《爱这个世界：汉娜·阿伦特传》，纽黑文：耶鲁大学出版社，2004年，第279页。
2. 引自伊丽莎白·扬－布鲁尔：《爱这个世界：汉娜·阿伦特传》，纽黑文：耶鲁大学出版社，2004年，第327页。
3. 扬－布鲁尔：《爱这个世界：汉娜·阿伦特传》，第 ix 页。

第三部分：学术影响

9 最初反响

要点 ⌖

- 对《人的境况》的批评主要集中在以下三个方面：对其他思想家思想的借鉴、阿伦特对概念的划分以及对"行动"的阐释。

- 阿伦特从未为了回应批评而改变自己的理论思想或研究方法，但她在之后的作品中尝试更清晰地阐释自己的核心思想。

- 对阿伦特著作的各种各样的批评，反映了当时知识分子界、意识形态、政治等多个领域的分歧。

批评

1958 年，《人的境况》发表。之后的几年里，这本书受到广泛的关注和解读。评论家们既关注该书整体，也关注书中的具体概念。他们主要提出以下三个方面的质疑：阿伦特的研究方法、论述架构及借用其他思想家理论的方式。

一些批评家质疑阿伦特的研究方法，特别是她对古希腊思想的借鉴。美国政治哲学家谢尔顿·沃林在《汉娜·阿伦特：民主与政治》一文中指出，阿伦特对古文明*的借鉴是时代错置*，因为这不恰当地将对现代社会的期望置于古典时期的语境中；同时，这也是精英主义的一种论述。[1] 他认为，阿伦特没有充分认识雅典政治的复杂性，以及促进政治论辩的日常经济事务的重要性。

俄裔英国哲学家、政治理论家以赛亚·柏林*批评《人的境况》缺少结构性的论述。他认为阿伦特"没有进行论证，也没有进行严肃周密的哲学思考和历史思考。她写的都是一些形而上学的自由联想，句与句之间也缺乏逻辑联系。"[2] 阿伦特受其他哲学家启发，以一种复杂、非正统的论证方式，提出大量观点，但没有一个完整的理论框架，使阿伦特的理论很难被相当一部分人接受。学者们批评她对其他思想家过于独特的解读，认为她有意将其他思想家的观点强行纳入自己的观点和立场。[3]

阿伦特对概念的区分也引起了争议。这主要是由于她从各种不同的语境对概念进行阐发。例如，致力于追求性别平等文化研究的女权主义 * 理论家批评阿伦特将"社会问题"从"政治行动"中分离出去。德国政治理论家汉娜·皮特金 *[4] 指出，阿伦特对个人领域、私人领域的划分，以及她赋予二者之间的等级秩序，有可能使母亲的角色及家庭生活固定在私人领域，由此失去自由。马克思主义者指责阿伦特将经济因素、社会因素排除在政治领域之外，在政治讨论中忽视贫困和剥削问题，使人们无法对社会不公进行探讨。即使一些阿伦特的支持者，也认为这一批评是有道理的。

> "但是，我感觉自己在历史研究和政治分析中，很明显存在一些普遍的困惑，随着极权主义充分地发展，这些困惑日渐显现。我也知道，我没有能够清楚地解释自己用来分析说明政治学和历史学整个领域的一种非正统方法。这本书的困难之一就是它不属于任何学派，也没有使用任何被正式认可或广泛存在争议的理论工具。"
> —— 汉娜·阿伦特："对《极权主义的起源》的回应"，《政治学评论》

回应

阿伦特并没有就这些批评做出正面回应，但她根据一些批评家的意见来完善自己的观点。在《论革命》（1963）中，阿伦特阐释了过多强调"社会性"将如何引发冲突甚至暴力。为了说明这一点，她对比了美国大革命与法国大革命：1775 年至 1781 年发生的美国大革命最终成功，是因为它专注于政治；而发生于 1789 年至 1793 年的法国大革命却以失败告终，因为它是从不平等这样的社会问题中孕育而生的（虽然法国大革命创建了一套民主政治体系，但不久这套体系就崩溃了，并导致了 1799 年独裁者拿破仑的上台）。

在《过去与未来之间》（1968）一书中，阿伦特论证了自己的理论观点可以如何在教育、文化等具体的领域得到应用实践。《论暴力》（1970）中，她提出较为激进的权力理论，进一步深化了她在《人的境况》中已提出的政治行动观点。书中，阿伦特认为，权力并非是处于高位统治他人，在她看来这应称作暴力；相反，权力是民众协力，从而带来改变。她以此观点考察了越南战争（冷战期间，1964 年到 1973 年，美国与北越交战，双方均伤亡惨重）期间学生的示威游行活动。阿伦特虽然支持游行示威活动，但她也对学生的抗议活动提出了批评，认为有时抗议活动的重点放在了对学校管理的不满上，而非战争本身。

我们可以看到，阿伦特对权力的定义阐明了一种事实：政治行动不单单意味着一个英雄式人物的独自行动；政治行动应以一种通力合作的形式进行，这种形式或许可以带来新的政治观点与制度。

冲突与共识

近期，学界对阿伦特愈发感兴趣，将她作品的思想扩展到国际关系[5]（对国与国之间互动关系的研究）等领域进行阐释。人们正在赋予其政治思想新内涵。[6] 她已发表的著作再版发行，设在纽约巴德学院的汉娜·阿伦特研究中心使学者可以接触到更多其未发表的文章，从而为她的理论思想开辟了新的研究视角。[7] 目前学者们认为，阿伦特在提出不同于主流的政治分析模式方面发挥了重要作用。尽管阿伦特作品的影响力越来越大，但我们仍无法说，政治学家、学者们已完全认同她的思想。她独到的研究方法促使读者以批判的眼光看待她的观点，而非简单地接受。

《人的境况》是阿伦特将"世界的异化"的含义理论化的一次大胆尝试。如果我们希望通过行动让世界焕然一新，那就需要让公民与他人建立联系，并形成一种共同世界、共同生活的观念。阿伦特意识到，现代世界已经侵蚀了这种共性，因此她试图通过理论建构去修复这种共性；反过来，这些理论又使我们得以对抗世界的异化。这也是阿伦特的政治行动思想在提出半个多世纪后，仍具影响力的原因。

---

1. 谢尔顿·沃林："汉娜·阿伦特：民主与政治"，《杂家》第 60 期，1983 年春夏刊，第 3—19 页。
2. 雷敏·亚罕拜格鲁：《以赛亚·柏林谈话录》，伦敦：皮特·奥尔班出版社，1992 年，第 82 页。
3. 更多关于阿伦特的评论，见沃尔特·拉克尔："聚焦阿伦特：政治评论员汉娜·阿伦特"，《当代历史杂志》第 33 卷，1998 年第 4 期，第 483—496 页。
4. 汉娜·皮特金："公平：论私人与公共"，《政治理论》第 9 卷，1981 年第 3 期，第 327—352 页。

5. 《汉娜·阿伦特与国际关系：跨领域解读》，安东尼·F.兰格和约翰·威廉编，伦敦：帕尔格雷夫出版社，2005年。

6. 《汉娜·阿伦特：关键概念》，帕特里克·海登编，纽约：劳特利奇出版社，2014年。

7. 如汉娜·阿伦特：《责任与判断》，杰罗姆·科恩编，纽约：肖肯出版社，2005年；汉娜·阿伦特：《政治的应许》，杰罗姆·科恩编，纽约：肖肯出版社，2007年；汉娜·阿伦特：《理解文集：1930—1954》，纽约：肖肯出版社，2005年；汉娜·阿伦特：《犹太问题著作集》，杰罗姆·科恩编，纽约：肖肯出版社，2008年。

10 后续争议

要点 ⁀

- "诞生性"（政治行动创建新制度、新现实的潜能）的概念可用来解读创造性艺术。

- 尽管阿伦特从未根据自己的著作创建学术流派，但一大批独立思想家已探讨并运用了她的理论框架。

- 许多不同学科的学者都关注阿伦特的思想，其中最著名的是德国哲学家尤尔根·哈贝马斯。这再次印证了阿伦特论著的重要地位。

应用与问题

阿伦特在《人的境况》中提出的观点在许多领域引发了讨论。苏格兰教育家莫温娜·格里菲斯＊认为阿伦特的诞生性概念可应用于艺术领域。[1] 阿伦特有关人类事务的理论模型是依托于改变的，新人来到世上，逐渐发展成为可以实施行动的人，该模型即发生了改变。阿伦特强调人类经验中的诞生性甚于有死性，促使我们以最初诞生时的样子思考自己。具有诞生性这一事实使人们拥有独特的生命轨迹，这又使每一个人都变得独一无二。阿伦特补充这一观点，认为只有通过在世界中行动，并将自己展现在世界与他人面前，我们才能获得独特的生命体验。一切行动都有其结果，为了回应这些结果，我们要做出更多行动。

一系列的行动及其产生的结果，构成了一个人的一生，激发了人的创造力，使其创造新事物，不断开始新事业，这些能力对需要创造性的艺术家来说意义重大。某种意义上，艺术家是具有独创性的制造者。用阿伦特的话来说，他们是需要观众的演员——他们要在公共领域中行动。这样，行动与艺术工作通过诞生性有了密切关联：一切从无到有诞生的新事物，只有通过不断创造的能力，才能使世界感知自己的存在。

> "每当你写出了作品并将其公之于众，很显然每个人都有自由按照自己的意愿解读它，也本该如此。"
>
> —— 汉娜·阿伦特："对美国基督教伦理学学会的评论"

思想流派

尽管阿伦特的著作有许多追随者，但她一生都没有尝试依据自己作品中的思想来创建学术流派。不过，仍有两个学派的思想构建于《人的境况》基础上，但略有发挥。其中一个是协商民主*理论，以土耳其裔美国政治哲学家塞拉·本哈比*[2]和德国哲学家尤尔根·哈贝马斯[3]为代表人物。哈贝马斯借鉴阿伦特对行动与制作的区分，指出工作与他所称的"交往行为"之间的区别。他认为，"阿伦特最主要的哲学著作《人的境况》系统地更新了亚里士多德派*的行动概念。"[4]

争胜主义者（认为民主建立在一定程度的冲突之上）是另一派借鉴阿伦特思想的理论家，其中有美国女权主义理论家邦妮·宏妮格[5]和政治学家帕特奇·马克尔[6]。他们强调创建政治空间，关注政治互动本质中的内在冲突；对他们来说，意见上的分歧是民主的重要一环。

当代研究

《人的境况》对许多当代学者产生了影响。除了以上提到的两派民主思想最明显外，还有不同学科的当代理论家受到了阿伦特的影响。例如，阿伦特认为叙事在社会政治理论中不可或缺，这使新西兰人类学家迈克尔·D. 杰克逊*受到启发，引用了阿伦特关于讲故事的著作来探索跨文化问题。[7]

在国际关系研究中，一批当代学者也受到阿伦特思想的深刻影响，如帕特里克·海登*、小安东尼·F. 兰格*、帕特丽夏·欧文斯、约翰·威廉姆斯等。他们在阿伦特的作品中发现了用新的方式看待全球政治的潜能，希望以此对抗全球性的无政府状态。此外，阿伦特的思想还为武力使用、战争犯罪、全球治理等问题带来新的解读。法学学者从阿伦特的作品中研究立法、宪法理论（通过法律定义一个国家的义务与本质的理论），他们认为阿伦特不仅是一位研究政治行动的理论家，也是一位立法的理论家，这尤其表现在她对立法的政治环境所做的叙述中。[8]

---

1. 见莫温娜·格里菲斯："研究与自我"，载《劳特利奇系列研究——艺术篇》，米歇尔·比格斯和亨利克·卡尔森编，牛津：劳特利奇出版社，2011 年，第 168 页。

2. 塞拉·本哈比：《汉娜·阿伦特："不情愿"的现代主义者》，加利福尼亚州，千橡市：世哲出版社，1996 年；《黑暗时代的政治：遇见汉娜·阿伦特》，塞拉·本哈比编，纽约：剑桥大学出版社，2010 年。

3. 尤尔根·哈贝马斯："阿伦特的权力交流观"，《社会研究》第 44 卷，1997 年第 1 号，春季刊，第 5 页。

4. 哈贝马斯："阿伦特的权力交流观"，第 5 页。

5. 邦妮·宏妮格：《政治理论及政治置换》，纽约州，伊萨卡：康奈尔大学出版社，

1993 年；《汉娜·阿伦特的女性主义解读》，邦妮·宏妮格编，宾夕法尼亚州，帕克：宾夕法尼亚大学出版社，1995 年。

6. 帕特奇·马克尔："人民的统治：阿伦特，本原和民主"，《美国政治科学评论》第 100 期第 1 号，2006 年，第 1—14 页。

7. 迈克尔·D.杰克逊：《政治叙说：暴力、犯罪和主体间性》，哥本哈根：图斯卡兰博物馆出版社，2002 年。

8. 克里斯蒂安·沃克：《阿伦特式宪政：法律、政治和自由秩序》，牛津：哈特出版社，2015 年。

11 当代印迹

要点 ⚷━

- 《人的境况》解答了为何政治抗议活动持续不断地发生，以及这些活动创建新制度的目标为何总是以失败告终。

- 《人的境况》的理论强调了"人的境况"的不可预知性，挑战了传统的分析方式；此外，阿伦特对概念的重新界定也质疑了分析现实的传统方式。

- 学界对阿伦特理论的探讨和批评丰富了对这部作品在原语境中解读的方式。

地位

在《人的境况》发表的半个多世纪后，这部作品仍是对政治理论、政治生活进行探讨时的热议对象。2000 年，研究阿伦特思想作品的论文集《剑桥阿伦特指南》出版，显示出她的思想在不同学科、不同视角下的重要性。[1] 在国际关系[2]、法学理论[3]等多种研究领域，阿伦特也颇具影响力。在这些论文中，《人的境况》提出的观点始终处于核心。

阿伦特在《人的境况》中提出的核心问题仍是当代政治论辩的焦点。她将社会性从政治性中分离出去，挑战了既有的思维方式；在这种区分的基础上，阿伦特重新思考了自由和政治行动。她的思想在当今的世界秩序中仍有重要意义，尤其是在世界各地爆发反新自由主义*经济（一种新型经济结构，主张社会资源私有化，阻止政府对市场的干预）的抗议活动的情况下。例如，自 2008 年金融危机爆发后，一些反资本主义组织在世界范围内掀起了占领运动*，这些占领运动正是阿伦特所说的政治行动的典型；民众发起的运动最终没有带来实质性的改变，正是因为这些抗议运动将注意力过多放在"社会性"事件上，而忽视了政治建制。

> "阿伦特钟爱西方的政治传统，但她没有用学院派的哲学论证方法，而是本着质疑与对话的精神，为当今寻找一个思想参照，我们仍可以通过阿伦特的作品来解答当今一些深层的政治问题。问题之一就是政治界限在社会中的变更，这也改变了公共领域与私人领域的划分。"
>
> —— 塞拉·本哈比："女性主义理论与汉娜·阿伦特公共空间的概念"，《人文科学史》

互动

阿伦特在书中阐释了社会性的兴起对政治性产生威胁的方式，这些观点至今仍不过时（例如，政治家错误地将国债与家庭债务相提并论）。但政治远不止如此，阿伦特认为，政治应创建一个充满平等与自由的民主空间。阿伦特有关"社会性蚕食了政治性"的观点对消费社会提出了尖锐的批评，这与自由派学者、马克思主义学者的观点背道而驰。政治论争大多围绕社会政策展开，尽量避免直接碰触政治议题。例如，虽然英国政党一直高声呼吁举行制宪会议（即召集人民代表共同起草制定宪法的会议），但是至今还没有举行过一次会议。这可能是因为英国政府专注于通过政治举措讨好选民，而非面对建立新制度、提出新理念的艰难任务。

2014 年，苏格兰举行了独立公投*（投票决定苏格兰是否脱英以获得独立），这是一次解决国家主权问题（显然是政治性问题）

的大胆尝试，在苏格兰激起许多政治对话。这些讨论说明阿伦特的政治思想至今仍有意义：人们不仅需要解决日常生活问题的社会政策，人们也想参与到对政治制度和政治理念的严肃讨论中。阿伦特的政治思想强调应对私人领域与公共领域、社会性与政治性进行划分，但仍然无法对界定划分时产生的冲突进行分析。她对劳动与行动的区分使她"在许多左派那里不受欢迎，但她对行动的解释却为各种民权运动＊中、铁幕＊背后的激进派人士传递了希望，带来了鼓舞人心的消息。"4（民权运动指与美国黑人平权相关的一系列社会运动；铁幕指 1945 至 1989 年间东欧与西欧间的分界线。）

持续争议

　　许多思想家批评阿伦特对私人／公共、社会性／政治性的划分过于机械。汉娜·皮特金等女权主义学者在其对文化的解读分析中重点关注性别不平等所带来的种种涵义，因此，她们批评《人的境况》忽视了性别议题。正如土耳其裔美国哲学家塞拉·本哈比所说："对于当代女权主义理论来说，汉娜·阿伦特的学术思想令人困惑，富有挑战性，但同时也令人气恼。"5 事实上，阿伦特对性别问题的立场远比起初显现出来的复杂。她将劳动定义为维持人类生活的活动；同时，劳动也满足人类饮食、消耗、繁殖等生理需求。这些活动在家庭等私人领域进行，生产的是必需品，因此人类在劳动中失去了自由。阿伦特默认将女性的母亲身份与劳动联系起来，因此女性受到了潜在的禁锢。但同时，对女性来说，诞生性（子女诞生）又意味着自由以及政治行动的新开始。

　　另一位对阿伦特的理论进行批评性探讨的学者是社会学家理查德·桑内特＊，他质疑阿伦特有关劳动的论述。《人的境况》对劳动者和技艺人进行等级划分，并认为前者不及后者。桑内特在《匠人》一书中批评了现实生活中这样的划分，认为匠人的活动要远远超越熟练手工劳动者的范围。

1. 《剑桥阿伦特指南》，德纳·维拉编，剑桥：剑桥大学出版社，2000年。
2. 《汉娜·阿伦特与国际关系：跨领域解读》，安东尼·F.兰格和约翰·威廉编，伦敦：帕尔格雷夫出版社，2006年；帕特丽夏·欧文斯：《战争与政治之间：国际关系与汉娜·阿伦特的思想》，牛津：牛津大学出版社，2008年；帕特里克·海登：《全球化时代的政治邪恶：阿伦特与国际关系理论》，伦敦：劳特利奇出版社，2009年。
3. 《汉娜·阿伦特与法律》，马尔科·格蒂尼和克里斯托夫·麦考金代尔编，牛津：哈特出版社，2012年。
4. 玛格丽特·加诺芬：《人的境况》导言，汉娜·阿伦特著，芝加哥：芝加哥大学出版社，1998年，第xv页。
5. 塞拉·本哈比："女性主义理论和汉娜·阿伦特的公共空间概念"，《人文科学史》第6期，1993年，第97页。

12 未来展望

要点 ⚬⟋

- 《人的境况》为我们提供新的视角，来解读政治抗议活动持续存在以及取得成功的原因。

- 阿伦特的学术思想极具原创性，应用广泛，这些特点使许多思想家在研究中借鉴了阿伦特的理论框架。

- 在《人的境况》中，阿伦特详细构建了自己独特的、非正统的理论框架，挑战了我们一直用来分析并理解政治的理论观点。

潜力

阿伦特的主张与她在《人的境况》中提出的观点在今天具有重要意义。她认为，"即使社会完全僵化，或向一种不可改变的方向发展，其中却依旧存在着新的开端。"[1] 对新开端的强调，潜在地赋予了抗议活动意义，而这也正是抗议活动取得成功的关键所在。对阿伦特而言，抗议活动是政治行动的核心，但如果仅限于关注不平等、贫困等社会问题，运动必将走向失败。她所理解的抗议运动，应是因社会事件而起，但之后抗议者要倾力于通过创建新体制来解决问题，从而取得最终的胜利。阿伦特为当今世界如何通过建制解决问题提供了见解。

阿伦特对政治不可预知性的思考及她所传递的希望有可能得到进一步发展。例如，她半个多世纪前对犹太复国主义（即希望在中东建立一个犹太国的政治运动）的著述，令人诧异地准确表述了当今世界正在面临的危险。阿伦特并不是简单地吁求人的行动；对她而言，没有一个人可以代表所有人采取行动，因为人是多元性的，每个人都是独特的个体。此外，她还强调创造力，认为希望孕育在新生命不断降生到世界的过程以及所带来的新的动力中。

> "站在新千年的门槛上，我们所能做的一个可靠预测就是，尽管已经开始的过程一直在持续，但开放的未来仍将成为无数人自发行动的舞台，这些自发行动远非我们当前所能想象。"
>
> —— 玛格丽特·加诺芬:《人的境况》导言

未来方向

阿伦特的理论帮助我们更好地理解当代发生的抗议运动，如2010年从中东国家蔓延开来的系列抗议运动（统称为"阿拉伯之春"）和2009年因伊朗人民不满总统选举而发生的伊朗绿色革命*。在这些抗议活动中，人们反抗的目标是一种僵化的官僚体系，但在阿伦特看来，以此作为目标将有害于政治生活。2011年，埃及人民在开罗解放广场进行抗议示威，最终建立了新的政治体制。但新的体制只关注社会秩序及政治治理实践，并未根本性地改变埃及的政治体制，因此以失败告终。此时，我们或许会回想起阿伦特的政治观点：政治行动并非永恒不变，而是一直在更新。阿伦特这种颇具革新性的对政治行动的解读，使个人事业服从于具有更重大意义的公共领域，这对我们理解当代政治既是一种挑战，也是一种贡献。此外，阿伦特就"地球的异化"发出了警告，因为"人类开启新事物的能力挑战了一切自然限制。"她也警惕"世界的异化"，因为"被更高效的生产和消费所独霸的现代自动化社会使我们仅仅像受自然法则支配的动物种群那样去行为和思考自身。"[2] 当今科学界及社会上热议的话题，如 DNA（遗传信息跨代传递的媒介）技术、核能、气候变化等，都彰显出阿伦特曾经的担忧是多么适用于当今时代。

小结

伊丽莎白·扬—布鲁尔在阿伦特的传记中，总结了阿伦特提出的核心问题："我们应如何严肃对待政治事件和政治领域？术语很简单，但问题却不好回答。"[3] 作为一部极具原创性的著作，《人的境况》为我们提供了反思政治与哲学的三个全新角度。首先，行动是创造与自由的根本性政治活动。其次，与之相对应，我们要明白行动具有潜在力量。最后，私人与公共之间，劳动、工作与行动之间都有概念上的划分。这三点改变了对政治的传统分析方法，意味着政治的研究领域发生了转换。阿伦特不再将政治局限在政府、体制中，而是扩展到行动，扩展到形形色色的人在公共领域的主动性上。对她来说，普遍的哲学原则无法用于指导政治领域，因为政治领域本身存在着哲学问题。她独树一帜地对以往的观点提出了全新的见解，以其另辟蹊径的研究方法，超越了传统的哲学研究，对我们用以分析、解读政治世界的话语提出了永久的挑战。

---

1. 玛格丽特·加诺芬：《人的境况》导言，汉娜·阿伦特著，芝加哥：芝加哥大学出版社，1998 年，第 xvii 页。

2. 加诺芬：《人的境况》导言，第 x—xi 页。

3. 伊丽莎白·扬-布鲁尔：《爱这个世界：汉娜·阿伦特传》，纽黑文：耶鲁大学出版社，2004 年，第 322 页。

术语表

1. **争胜主义**：政治理论术语，指强调分歧、辩论而非共识的民主形式，这些分歧争论不至带来暴力，而是有利于政治生活。

2. **美国革命**：1775年，由美国殖民者发起的革命运动，反抗英国政府的统治；1781年，革命结束，最终北美十三个州的殖民地脱离大英帝国，建立了美利坚合众国。

3. **时代错置**：对历史术语进行现代意义的阐释，过程中忽视了不同时代之间的差异。例如，将当代英国的"民主"概念应用到古雅典的论述上，即可视为一种"时代错置"。

4. **分析哲学**：一种哲学流派，常见于英美大学中，注重通过逻辑分析来阐明意义，而不是形而上学的思辨。

5. **古希腊**：公元前8世纪到公元前6世纪期间的希腊文明。

6. **古文明**：通常用来指中世纪前的"古典的"古代文明，特别是古希腊文明、罗马文明。

7. **反犹主义**：对犹太人的敌意、歧视、偏见或憎恨。

8. **阿拉伯之春**：指2010年发生在阿拉伯世界的暴力及非暴力抗议、游行示威、内战等系列运动。

9. **亚里士多德派**：以古希腊哲学家亚里士多德（公元前384—前322年）理论思想为基础的哲学流派。

10. **行为主义**：一种社会学思想，强调分析人的行为，而非一味关注制度、思想。研究方法上多使用数据分析、定量分析。

11. **资本主义**：一种经济体制，以私有制、私企、利润最大化为根基。

12. **非暴力反抗**：运用和平、冷静的方式对政府表达抗议；抗议者事先默认自己将受到政府的惩处。

13. **民权运动**：与美国黑人平权相关的一系列社会运动。

14. **冷战**：西方国家与东方共产主义国家关系紧张的时期。自 20 世纪 40 年代后期（第二次世界大战后）开始，到 20 世纪 90 年代前期随着柏林墙的倒塌结束。

15. **殖民主义**：一国对另一国进行统治；殖民国与被殖民国之间关系不平等，殖民国通过对被殖民国的资源掠夺，来增强本国的经济实力。

16. **集中营/死亡营**：第二次世界大战期间，德国纳粹政府设立的营地，用来关押犹太人、同性恋、持不同政见者及其他一些被视为不良分子的人。

17. **充分条件**：拉丁语，意为"某一条件是充分的"。

18. **必要条件**：拉丁语，意为"某一条件是必要的"（即若无某一条件为前提，则不成立）。

19. **沉思哲学**：重视沉思、思考甚于行动的哲学传统。

20. **欧陆哲学**：以法国、德国为主的哲学流派，重视史料，探索广义的形而上学问题。

21. **偶然性**：指无法预知行动的结果。

22. **去殖民化**：被殖民国家争取独立的过程。

23. **协商民主**：认为在一个真正的民主国家中，只有投票选举是不够的，协商是民主决策的重要一环。

24. **经验主义**：指某事可通过观察得到证实。

25. **存在主义**：无神论的哲学流派，强调宇宙与现实都缺少秩序，与 20 世纪法国哲学家阿尔贝·加缪、让—保罗·萨特等人的哲学思想相近。

26. **女权主义**：通过性别视角进行社会分析的思想流派，旨在实现男女两性在文化、政治、经济上的平等。

27. **法国大革命**：法国社会各阶层共同发起的革命运动，起于 1789 年；1793 年，波旁王朝国王路易十六被公开处死，标志着法国大革命的结束。大革命后一段时间内，法国建立起相对公平的社会，直到 1804 年拿破仑·波拿巴执政。

28. **原教旨主义者**：原教旨主义起源于 19 世纪的基督教神学，原教旨主义者希望信仰体系回归到原初状态或最重要的宗教传统元素中。这意味着对宗教文本进行字面上的解读。现在"原教旨主义者"指通过字面意义解读宗教文本、对宗教持保守态度的宗教信仰者。

29. **绿色革命**：因 2009 年伊朗总统选举引起的一系列抗议运动，抗议当时的总统马哈茂德·艾哈迈迪内贾德再次当选。

30. **古根海姆基金会**：美国慈善基金会，为社会科学和人文领域的研究提供赞助。

31. **黑格尔派**：运用哲学家黑格尔的思想进行哲学分析。这种哲学分析方法吸收了黑格尔唯心主义的观点，关注理性如何主宰现实。

32. **唯心主义**：以理念作为世界本原，轻视物质现实的哲学传统。

33. **帝国主义**：指某国在外交政策上企图建立殖民地，对其他国家进行殖民统治。帝国主义可用来指通俗意义上的帝国，如罗马帝国；也可用来指非传统意义上的帝国，如当今的美国。

34. **铁幕**：通常用来指 1945 年至 1989 年间东欧与西欧之间的分界线。

35. **自由主义**：倡导个体自由，以非暴力的方式进行政治、社会及经济体制变革。

36. **自由多元主义**：自由主义政治理论的一种思想，认为只要不对他人有害，道德、宗教信仰都应为社会所接受。

37. **马克思主义**：19 世纪中后期，政治哲学家卡尔·马克思与社会学家弗里德里希·恩格斯共同提出的一套政治经济理论，马克思理论从经济学的角度解读社会变迁，并预言无产阶级革命将推翻资本主义。

38. **形而上学**：一种哲学研究，目的在于用最基本的方式认识存在事物的本质。

39. **诞生性**：阿伦特使用的哲学术语，用来指通过政治行动完成建制、创造新现实的可能性；但是诞生性也可能带来意料之外的现实，就像没有人可以预知一个孩子会成长为怎样的人，也没有人能预知政治行动会产生怎样的结果。

40. **民族主义**：一种政治意识形态，认为爱国是最重要的政治准则，这一意识形态反映出一种思想，即人类从自己国家文化、社会、政治中的受益，远多于从普遍原则、国际机构之中的受益。

41. **纳粹主义**：纳粹党的意识形态，纳粹党在 1933 年至 1945 年间统治德国。纳粹主义是各种法西斯主义的集合，包括种族主义、反犹主义、民族主义及国家殖民扩张。

42. **新自由主义**：新兴起的一种自由主义（以 20 世纪八九十年代为主）。新自由主义认同个体的自由选择，同时认为政府应尽量少地干预经济社会生活。

43. **客观主义**：一种哲学理论，认为现实独立存在于人类思想之外。

44. **占领运动**：2008 年世界金融危机爆发后，发生在世界各地的反资本主义的抗议活动。

45. **现象学**：对主观经验、意识进行结构分析的哲学研究。德国哲学家埃德蒙德·胡塞尔创建了这一哲学流派。

46. **柏拉图式真理**：产生自古希腊哲学家柏拉图的哲学思想，认为"真理"存在于理念世界中。柏拉图哲学的根基是认为每一事物都有一个理念存在，帮助我们定义客体、确立体制，并指导现实生活实践。

47. **多元主义**：认为有多种不同的存在方式，它们都应受到尊重。与宽容不同，宽容意味着我们要无条件接受他人观点。多元主义方法提出，多种不同观点、看法是有益的。

48. **实证主义**：一种哲学思想，认为事实只能通过数据、科学方法、客观主义来认识。

49. **行动 / 制作**：古希腊语 praxis，意为"行动"。在阿伦特看来，行动是积极生活的最重要形式。阿伦特借鉴了亚里士多德对行动（praxis）和制作（poiesis）的划分，在其理论思想中具体阐释了"行动"概念的特征。

50. **抵抗运动**：指以暴力或非暴力的方式抵抗纳粹的占领，尤其指第二次世界大战期间法国的抵抗运动。

51. **苏格兰公投（2014）**：2014 年，苏格兰政府举行独立公投，旨在脱英独立。公投结果决定苏格兰仍属英国管辖。

52. **世俗的**：形容某一政治体制或社会在方方面面不以宗教为主导。

53. **社会民主党**：一种政治立场，既认同自由民主，又在财富再分配问题上持社会主义立场。

54. **苏维埃社会主义共和国联盟（苏联）**：1922 年至 1991 年间，横跨欧亚大陆的一个社会主义国家。

55. **人造卫星"伴侣号"**：1957 年 10 月 4 日，苏联发射的人类第一颗人造卫星。

56. **极权主义**：一种政治体制，中央政府对社会施加绝对的权威，控制民众的私人生活和公共生活，并且要民众绝对服从。

57. **超验**：指不可被观察到、经验无法验证的现实，常用来形容个体的宗教体验——个体感受到与神之间的某种联系。

58. **越南战争（1961—1975）**：美国与北越之间发生的战争，美国借此保卫自己名义上的盟友——南越。美国国内对这场战争有大量反对的声音，越南战争也是美国历史上极少数以失败告终的战争之一。

59. **积极生活 / 沉思生活**："积极生活"指一种行动的生活，与之相反的是"沉思生活"，指一种投入冥想、思考的生活。尽管在哲学传统中，思想家将"沉思生活"置于更高位置，但对阿伦特而言，"积极生活"更适应于人的境况。

60. **第二次世界大战**（1939—1945）：一场全球规模的战争，战争双方为以德国、意大利、日本等国形成的轴心国和英国及其殖民地、苏联、美国等形成的同盟国，以同盟国获胜告终。

61. **犹太复国主义**：犹太人发起的民族主义政治运动，将以色列视为犹太人民的理想家园。

人名表

1. 亚里士多德（前384—前322），古希腊哲学家，柏拉图的学生。他被视为西方哲学的奠基者，其著作涵盖诸多学科领域，如物理、生物、逻辑、伦理学、美学、诗歌、戏剧、音乐、政治等。

2. 希波的奥古斯丁（354—430），北非的基督教神学家、哲学家。他在作品《上帝之城》中，试图调和罗马帝国与基督教的矛盾，强调政治秩序在精神生活中的重要性。

3. 塞拉·本哈比（1950年生），耶鲁大学政治哲学家，专事研究阿伦特和哈贝马斯，以女性主义批判理论闻名。其阿伦特研究专著有《汉娜·阿伦特："不情愿"的现代主义者》（1996）。

4. 以赛亚·伯林（1909—1997），哲学家、社会政治理论家、评论家及历史思想家。他曾在牛津大学任教，为自由主义辩护，抨击政治极端主义和狂热思想。代表作有《两种自由概念》（1958）。

5. 海因里希·布吕赫（1899—1970），德国诗人、哲学家。他使妻子汉娜·阿伦特对马克思主义理论产生研究兴趣。

6. 玛格丽特·加诺芬（1939年生），英国政治理论家，阿伦特研究专家。她在英国基尔大学教授政治思想。其阿伦特研究专著有《阿伦特政治思想重释》（1994）。

7. 伯纳德·克里克（1928—2008），英国政治学家，研究公共伦理及政治学。

8. 戴维·伊斯顿（1906—1962），加拿大政治学家，一生中的大多数时间都在美国任教，将行为主义视为政治研究的重要途径。

9. 阿道夫·艾希曼（1906—1962），纳粹高官，负责将欧洲的犹太人运往集中营。第二次世界大战后逃往阿根廷，后被以色列政府逮捕，接受审判，最终判处死刑。

10. 约翰·肯尼思·加尔布雷思（1908—2006），加拿大经济学家和外交

官员，是自由主义的坚定拥护者。

11. 莫温娜·格里菲斯（1948 年生），爱丁堡大学教育学教授，从事哲学、教育的写作。

12. 尤尔根·哈贝马斯（1929 年生），极具影响力的德国哲学家、社会学家，他一生对社会政治理论、认识论及实用主义研究做出了杰出贡献，代表作有《交往行为理论》（1981）。

13. 帕特里克·海登（1965 年生），国际知名政治理论家，任教于圣·安德鲁斯大学。

14. 格奥尔格·W. F. 黑格尔（1770—1831），德国哲学家，认为理念决定现实。黑格尔提出了辩证法，即对立理念经互动来创造现代社会的过程。黑格尔思想影响了卡尔·马克思等诸多哲学家的思想创作。

15. 马丁·海德格尔（1889—1976），极具影响力的德国哲学家，主要致力于现象学、存在主义的研究，探索存在的问题。1927 年，发表著作《存在与时间》，被学界公认为是 20 世纪最重要的哲学著作。第三帝国（即希特勒统治下的德国）兴起前的一段时间里，海德格尔与阿伦特产生了恋情。

16. 埃德蒙德·胡塞尔（1859—1938），在创建现象学派哲学过程中起重要作用，关注对主观经验、意识本质的结构性分析。代表作有《逻辑研究》（1900—1901）。

17. 迈克尔·D. 杰克逊（1940 年生），新西兰的诗人、人类学家，也是存在主义人类学创始人。代表作有《讲述的政治》（2002）。

18. 卡尔·雅斯贝斯（1883—1969），德国哲学家，其思想在现代神学、精神病学、哲学领域产生影响，代表作有《哲学》（1932）。

19. 拿撒勒耶稣（约公元前 4 年—约公元 30 年），犹太先知，居住在罗马帝国统治下的巴勒斯坦，是基督教的创始人。

20. 伊曼努尔·康德（1724—1804），德国启蒙哲学家，旨在将理性与经验统一起来，代表作有《纯粹理性批判》（1781）。

21. **小安东尼·F. 兰格**（1968 年生），国际知名政治理论家，在圣·安德鲁斯大学任教。

22. **卡尔·马克思**（1818—1883），德国哲学家，社会主义革命者。1848年，马克思与弗里德里希·恩格斯合写了著作《共产党宣言》，发展出一套政治经济理论，后被称为马克思主义。马克思主义的核心思想是从经济学的角度阐释社会变迁，并预言无产阶级革命将推翻资本主义统治。

23. **查理·梅里亚姆**（1874—1953），美国政治学家，在芝加哥大学进行学术研究，他是行为主义的倡导者，主张用实际可行的方法解决美国的政治问题。

24. **汉娜·皮特金**（1931 年生），加利福尼亚大学伯克利分校政治学教授，因对"代表"概念的论述而闻名。著作有《代表的概念》（1967）、《对异端的攻击：汉娜·阿伦特的"社会"概念》（1998）。

25. **柏拉图**（公元前 428/7 年—公元前 348/7 年），古希腊哲学家，雅典学院的创始人，与苏格拉底、亚里士多德同为西方哲学的奠基人。

26. **卡尔·波普尔**（1902—1994），奥地利哲学家，20 世纪最著名的科学哲学家之一。

27. **约翰·罗尔斯**（1921—2002），美国伦理学家，政治学家，在著作《正义论》（1971）中，提出"公平的正义"理论，回应了民主国家公民对自由、平等的呼求。

28. **W. W. 罗斯托**（1916—2003），美国政治理论家、经济学家。罗斯托因其保守的政治观点闻名，如他反对共产主义，支持资本主义、越南战争。

29. **理查德·桑内特**（1943 年生），社会学家，曾任伦敦政治经济学院和纽约大学的教授，研究城市中的社会关系、都市生活对个体的影响。代表作有《匠人》（2008）。

30. **路德维希·维特根斯坦**（1889—1951），哲学家，出生于奥地利，但主要在英国工作。维特根斯坦去世后，其学生伊丽莎白·安斯康姆将其作品审订并译成英文，出版《哲学研究》（1953），这一巨著对

20 世纪英国哲学产生了巨大影响。

31. **谢尔顿·沃林**（1922—2015），美国政治理论家，他在他最著名的作品《政治学与愿景》中认为，政治应避免追求宏伟的愿景，更应重视民主实践。

32. **伊丽莎白·扬—布鲁尔**（1946—2011），从事阿伦特研究的美国学者、心理治疗师。其著名的阿伦特研究著作是《爱这个世界：汉娜·阿伦特传》（2004）。

WAYS IN TO THE TEXT

- German-born Hannah Arendt (1906–75) immigrated to the United States during World War II* (1939–45). Her work profoundly shaped modern political theory.

- Her book *The Human Condition* (1958) emphasizes political action and pluralism* (the idea that the various possible ways of being in the world should be respected); both remain central to politics today.

- *The Human Condition* argues that politics creates and recreates institutions that allow for democratic participation.

Who Was Hannah Arendt?

Born in Germany in 1906, Hannah Arendt, the author of *The Human Condition* (1958), was one of the most influential political thinkers of the twentieth century. She studied philosophy with important figures such as Martin Heidegger,* the author of the renowned work *Being and Time* (1927), and Karl Jaspers,* the influential author of *Philosophy* (1932). As a Jew, she was forced to leave Germany in 1933 when the ruling Nazi* Party refused to allow Jews to hold meaningful jobs. She spent some time in Paris supporting Jews who were trying to immigrate to Palestine. After a brief internment in a French refugee camp, she eventually moved to the United States with her husband, Heinrich Blucher,* a philosopher and Marxist* thinker. Marxism is a set of political and economic theories developed in the mid to late nineteenth century; it explains social change in terms of economics, and predicts a workers' revolution that will overthrow the social and economic system of capitalism.* Arendt and Blucher worked primarily in New York city.

Arendt published books and essays on topics such as revolution, political action, freedom, power, and authority. Providing the theoretical foundation for her overall approach to political life, *The Human Condition* (1958) remains the most important of her works— but not just in terms of understanding Arendt. The text emphasizes action over passivity in political life. Instead of seeing politics as being about governments serving the people, Arendt argues that true politics is about active citizenship. Individuals must come together to recreate their institutions through constant action, such as revolutions or political protests.

Arendt first came to the attention of the reading public with the publication of *The Origins of Totalitarianism* in 1951. After *The Human Condition*, she wrote a number of other influential works. In 1961, the *New Yorker* magazine asked her to report on the war crimes trial of the Nazi bureaucrat Adolf Eichmann,* who was charged with organizing the transportation of Jewish people to concentration camps*, and who was tried in Israel. She expanded the article into a book, *Eichmann in Jerusalem* (1963). In it, she coined the phrase "the banality of evil" to describe how unthinking bureaucrats could sanction horrific events. She also described how the Nazi bureaucracy used European Jewish community institutions to facilitate the transfer of Jews to their deaths. This caused a great deal of controversy among Jewish readers. In 1963, she published *On Revolution,* an influential comparison of the American Revolution* of 1775–81, which ended with the establishment of the United States, and the French Revolution* of 1789–93, which saw the overthrow of the monarchy and the creation of a republic. She also wrote significant essays about civil disobedience* (action, usually peaceful but unlawful, taken to protest against a government), violence, power, and authority. In her later years, Arendt turned to what she called "the life of the mind," seeking to understand three things: thinking, willing, and judging. She died in 1975 at the age of 69 while writing about the final subject, judging.

What Does *The Human Condition* Say?

The Human Condition proposes that human life is defined by three kinds of activity: labor, work, and action. Labor includes what we do to support our daily needs, such as feeding ourselves. Work includes things that will outlive our immediate lives, such as science, art, and literature. Action remains the quintessentially political form of activity; it allows us to work together to shape our common destiny. Arendt believed action to be important and all too neglected in our understanding of "normal politics." While some see political life as being about purely economic schemes or social debates, Arendt believed politics should primarily be about how people work in unison to create new institutions. These new institutions in turn create spaces in which we can reveal ourselves in public to each other.

The book is an example of what is called a phenomenological* approach to politics. Phenomenology is a philosophical study of the structures of subjective experience and consciousness ("subjective experience" here means, simply, experience belonging uniquely to an individual). *The Human Condition* focuses on the realm of appearances, rather than a search for some fundamental truth about human life or politics. Action, which Arendt saw as the most important form of human activity, is partly about creating new institutions. But it is also about revealing ourselves to each other in a commonly constructed political space.

Modern politics too often neglects this activity of public revelation, or misunderstands it, thinking it means revealing things about our personal lives. But Arendt would label our personal lives as belonging to the social realm rather than the political realm. Revealing ourselves in political life means advancing ideas and creating institutions through which we can accept a plurality of visions of how politics should function. Pluralism is the idea that there are many different ways of being in the world, that they should all be respected, and that we can benefit from these alternative views and ideas.

The book also draws heavily on a particular reading of the ancient Greek* experience—both the history of democracy as we understand it from its origins in the Greek city of Athens, and the ideas of the Greek philosopher Aristotle.* Aristotle defined human beings as thinking, political actors. Arendt emphasized the political element of human life even more than the thinking part. This suggests she believed philosophers like the Greek philosopher Plato,* who saw humans as primarily thinkers, to have been mistaken.

The Human Condition argues against Marxist theories. Arendt believed they focused too much attention on the realm of labor, while neglecting the realm of political action. The book also positions itself against forms of the political philosophy of liberalism,* which see politics as being about giving maximum freedom to individuals to pursue their personal interests. Arendt did believe in the protection of a private space for individuals, but she also believed that politics should be about acting together and becoming proud citizens of our respective countries.

The book introduces or redefines important concepts. The idea of plurality, for instance, represents more than liberal pluralism.* It focuses more on creating spaces for a large number of different forms of citizen engagement. Arendt also created the idea of natality,* the idea that politics always centers on giving birth to new institutions and ideas.

The book begins and ends by reminding us that we are bound to this planet. Our human existence cannot be about afterlives or other worlds. Instead, we must focus our politics in the here and now. Doing so will give us the means to continually improve *the human condition* as we create new spaces and institutions to make our common life easier.

Why Does *The Human Condition* Matter?

The Human Condition remains just as relevant today as it was in 1958. The totalitarian* regimes of Nazi Germany that concerned Arendt so much during her lifetime may have now disappeared—totalitarianism is a political system in which the centralized government holds total authority over society, controls private and public life, and requires complete subservience—but in the twenty-first century, states and multinational companies govern and control us through surveillance and technology. These forms of control turn us into passive consumers. *The Human Condition* reminds us how important it is to be active, to *engage* in a life of politics in which we can resist things we don't want or like, and create new institutions. The book emphasizes the benefits of political activism, such as the popular revolts in the Middle East of 2010 collectively known as the Arab Spring.* Even when those movements collapse or fail, they are examples of *the human condition* of continual striving to resist and to create new political institutions and ideas.

The Human Condition's emphasis on the world of appearances (abstract subjective experiences rather than fundamental truths) also makes it relevant today. A focus on the otherworldly concerns of religions has crept into politics in many regions of the world. Arendt believed, rather, that we are bound by the earth on which we live. That means we must act together to succeed in navigating the tensions that arise from living in a crowded space. Instead of hoping for utopias either here or elsewhere, we must conduct politics in *this* world. That means creating space for disagreement and conflict in ways that do not lead to violence.

Finally, and connected to the last point, Arendt's emphasis on plurality and respect for others helps the work move past simple liberal platitudes about accepting others, and toward a more active approach to shaping politics. Unlike tolerance, which means grudgingly accepting others, pluralism means actively embracing differences and appreciating others for what they can bring to politics. Arendt's work reminds us of how important it is not simply to tolerate difference, but to embrace plurality.

SECTION 1
INFLUENCES

MODULE 1
THE AUTHOR AND THE HISTORICAL CONTEXT

KEY POINTS

* Hannah Arendt's *The Human Condition* helps us see the importance of political action in the face of forces that seek to limit our engagement with the world and with each other.

* *The Human Condition* arose from the author's education as a student of German philosophy in the early twentieth century, and from her experience of being a Jew in Nazi* Germany.

* *The Human Condition* continued her work on totalitarianism* (a political system with a domineering centralized government) and articulates an idea of politics that emphasizes action as the defining element of *the human condition*.

Why Read This Text?

Hannah Arendt's *The Human Condition* (1958) remains an important text more than half a century after its publication. While politics can lead to conflict, Arendt emphasized the plurality* of our life on this earth: we can benefit, she argues, from alternative views and ideas, and we must respect and work with others to create new political institutions. Both religious and secular* fundamentalist* ideologies (belief systems that seek to return to the "fundamentals" or most important elements of a tradition) fail to acknowledge this plurality. They assume that we possess only one human nature, which can be molded to create perfection. Arendt reminds us that while we share the earth, we do not share a single human nature.

We must remake ourselves anew with each generation.

For Arendt, general philosophical principles cannot regulate the political domain. She seeks to reform political theory by underlining the contingency* of human life, and especially by defining action as the central concept of politics. "Contingency" is the idea that we cannot predict the possible outcome of any course of action. Arendt wrote *The Human Condition* in the aftermath of World War II,* when the world needed a new approach to politics. She brought a message of hope—that people remain active beings and that action enables us to create new things—that is still relevant today. Her work serves as a "reminder of the vital importance of politics, and of properly understanding our political capacities and the dangers and opportunities they offer."[1]

> *"In the early 1950s Hannah Arendt began to envision a new science of politics for a world in which political events, world wars, totalitarianism, and atomic bombing demanded serious attention from philosophers."*
>
> —— Elisabeth Young-Bruehl, *Hannah Arendt: For Love of the World*

Author's Life

Arendt was born in 1906 in the city of Linden (now Hanover) to a social democrat* family of secular German Jews; social democrats subscribe to liberal* principles of democracy and endorse economic policies that allow the fair distribution of wealth. She enrolled at Marburg University in 1924 to study under the influential German philosopher Martin Heidegger.* Arendt's education, with its focus on ancient history and philosophy, shaped her thinking. In 1926, she completed a doctoral degree in philosophy at Heidelberg University. The German Swiss philosopher Karl Jaspers* supervised her dissertation on the idea of love in the work of the early Christian theologian Augustine of Hippo.*

Partly because of the growth of anti-Semitism*—hostility and discrimination towards Jewish people—in Germany during her university years, Arendt's Jewish identity became more central to her thinking, and she associated herself with some Jewish and Zionist* organizations; Zionism is a nationalist and political movement that sees the land of Israel as the rightful homeland of the Jewish people.[2]

In 1933, the rise of Nazism forced Arendt to move to Paris, where she supported efforts to help Jews escape Europe, and worked in the resistance* (organizations that worked, violently and nonviolently, against the German occupation). After being imprisoned in 1941, Arendt escaped to the United States. She briefly returned to Germany at the end of the war to continue supporting Jewish refugees. She then returned to the United States, eventually becoming a US citizen. She and her husband Heinrich Blucher,* a philosopher and Marxist* thinker, lived largely in NewYork city, but Arendt taught at universities across the country and lectured widely around the world.

Author's Background

Hannah Arendt's upbringing as a German Jew profoundly shaped her interest in politics, authority, and power. Her two early works—*The*

Origins of Totalitarianism (1952) and *The Human Condition* (1958)—arose from her efforts to come to terms with the horrific events of two world wars. For her, the totalitarianism of Nazism represented the end of common and plural life, and the death of politics.

Her identity as a Jew shaped her 1963 book *Eichmann in Jerusalem*. After originally believing that Israel represented hope for the Jewish people, she became disillusioned by the way in which the Jewish state continued to use the mass murder of European Jews by the Nazis for nationalist* purposes. Her engagement with US political thought partly shaped her work *On Revolution* (1963). In her collection of essays *Crises of the Republic* (1970), she analyzed America's imperialist* foreign policy (that is, the US policy of extending its sphere of cultural and economic influence beyond its own shores) in the Vietnam War,* and examined how citizens should respond to it. The best-known essay in the collection, "On Violence," examines the decolonization* period, when former colonies of the European powers sought their independence. This took place largely in Africa, but Middle East and Asian colonies also sought independence during this period. It also looks at attempts by figures in the United States and elsewhere to justify violence in the context of revolution.

---

1. Hannah Arendt, *The Human Condition*, introduced by Margaret Canovan (Chicago: University of Chicago Press, 1998), xvi.

2. Some of her writings on Zionism and Judaism can be found in Hannah Arendt, *The Jewish Writings*, eds. Jerome Kohn and Ron H. Feldman (New York: Random House, 2006).

ACADEMIC CONTEXT

KEY POINTS

* Philosophy deals with understanding reality and existence.

* Contemplative philosophy,* an abstract and theoretical approach, has long been considered the best way to understand reality.

* Arendt rejects classical contemplative philosophy for a more active and concrete mode of thought. She underlines this rupture by calling herself a political theorist rather than a political philosopher.

The Work in Its Context

Hannah Arendt published *The Human Condition* in 1958. The field of philosophy had been consistently dominated by a contemplative tradition that started with the ancient Greek* philosopher Plato.* Contemplative philosophy focuses on the life of the mind and prizes theoretical reflection over political action. This approach seeks a transcendental* truth (a term used to describe a reality that is beyond the observable or empirically verifiable) to explain the world. It considers thought the most valuable activity a person can engage in.

During Arendt's lifetime, most philosophers adopted one of two styles: analytic philosophy* or continental philosophy.*[1] To simplify the distinctions we can say that analytical philosophers think about reality with conceptual and argumentative clarity, objectivism* (the assumption that the mind and reality are independent), and logic. They often identify with the sciences and mathematics, rather than with the humanities. The foundational key figures of this tradition include the Austrian British philosopher Ludwig Wittgenstein* and the American John Rawls.* In contrast, the theories of continental philosophers tend to be more literary and less analytical, and more interested in political, cultural, and metaphysical* issues (that is, abstract issues concerning the nature of reality, time, and so on). These philosophers often work from a historical perspective. Scholars usually consider the early nineteenth-century German philosopher Georg Wilhelm Friedrich Hegel* to have been the founder of this approach.

Other key figures (all German) in continental philosophy included the nineteenth-century founder of socialism, Karl Marx;* the philosopher Edmund Husserl,* whose work straddled the nineteenth and twentieth centuries; Martin Heidegger;* and Jürgen Habermas.* Analytic philosophy dominated in English-speaking countries during the twentieth century. As the name implies, philosophers throughout Europe more commonly practiced continental philosophy. But the geographical divide is misleading. The main differences between the two approaches lay in their methods and approaches.

> "The Human Condition *questions the major Western tradition from Plato to Marx which sees humans coming to the full realization of their potential in the theoretical life. For Arendt this emphasis on the theoretical is a betrayal of the practical."*
> —— Dermot Moran, *Introduction to Phenomenology*

Overview of the Field

In the 1950s, when Arendt was working on *The Human Condition*, the analytical/continental debate turned into a debate between positivism* and phenomenology.*

In philosophy, positivism values empirical* data (that is, information acquired through observation) and scientific methods over metaphysical speculations. From a positivist perspective, we find truth by observing and interpreting factual data. Phenomenology, on the other hand, assumes that we cannot find truth by this means. Rather, all we have are "phenomena," or appearances. So we must focus on our subjective experiences, and the best we can do is understand reality as it appears to us. This philosophical tradition does not deny the existence of reality, but it suggests that simply "observing" and calculating will not reveal truths to us in the way that positivists believe they will.

Besides this classical split, ideological trends also divided the philosophical field. In the 1950s, the world was at the beginning of what would become a half-century of Cold War* struggle, a tense nuclear standoff between two superpowers—the US against the Soviet Union.* This confrontation colored scholarship in many areas, including the social sciences. Indeed, the confrontation between liberal* traditions and Marxist* theories heavily influenced the ways in which scholars defined and answered philosophical problems. For instance, the liberal tradition usually speaks of individual freedoms (economic, social, and political). In Marxist theory, individuals find fulfillment via communal action designed to change the economic structures that surround us.

Academic Influences

According to the English political theorist Margaret Canovan,* Arendt paid "no attention to mainstream debates" and always distrusted philosophical schools.[2] But in *The Human Condition* she drew on three of the greatest German philosophers of the twentieth century: Heidegger, Husserl, and Karl Jaspers.* In emphasizing the potential for political action to change the world around us, she drew on the phenomenological influences of Heidegger and Husserl. Like them, Arendt believed that we live in a world of appearances, so our actions can shape and reshape the world in fundamental ways. She shared Heidegger's perspective of "being in the world," which he had developed in his 1927 masterwork *Being and Time*.[3] Heidegger emphasized the importance of humans' interactions with their environment; but Arendt criticized his neglect of the cooperative dimension of human activity, because for her the world existed "between" people.[4] She rarely characterized herself as a phenomenologist, but we can understand her work as an offshoot of this tradition.

In criticizing the contemplative tradition of philosophy, Arendt echoed Jaspers, who shared her tendency to gravitate toward a concrete and practical philosophy. Jaspers introduced her to the eighteenth-century German philosopher Immanuel Kant's* reflection on politics. This led her to engage critically with ancient philosophers. She rejected Plato's political philosophy because it suggested—incorrectly, she thought—that philosophy remains superior to politics. Instead, she preferred Aristotle; in combining the active and philosophical life, she found his approach closer to her own. But Arendt went further than Aristotle in arguing for a politics of action above all else. She wanted to go beyond the contemplative tradition and renew thinking on politics. This contradicted both the predominant approach of American philosophers and mainstream European philosophy. She accused the latter of being incapable of understanding *the human condition* because it produced models disconnected from action. As a result, in the words of her biographer, "she had a deep suspicion of Hegelian* and Marxist attempts to explain the overall meaning of the historical as such."[5] ("Hegelian" refers to the philosophical approach of Hegel, focusing on how ideas determine our reality.)

This explains why Arendt was reluctant to call herself a philosopher and preferred the term "political theorist" or "political thinker."[6]

---

1. See Carl E. Schorske, "The New Rigorism in the Human Sciences, 1940–1960," *Daedelus* 126, no. 1 (1997): 289–310; and Brian Leiter and Michael Rosen, eds., *The Oxford Handbook of Continental Philosophy* (Oxford: Oxford University Press, 2007).

2. Margaret Canovan, introduction to *The Human Condition* by Hannah Arendt (Chicago: University of Chicago Press, 1998), xv.

3. Martin Heidegger, *Being and Time* (New York: Harper, 1962).

4. Hannah Arendt, *The Human Condition* (Chicago: University of Chicago Press, 1998), 52.

5. Dermot Moran, *Introduction to Phenomenology* (London & New York: Routledge, 2000), 290.

6. Elisabeth Young-Bruehl, *Hannah Arendt: For Love of the World* (New Haven: Yale University Press, 2004), 327.

MODULE 3
THE PROBLEM

KEY POINTS

* Arendt is concerned with the rise of the "social"—the idea that managerial and bureaucratic solutions can address all our problems.

* Politics should not be a matter of mere "housekeeping." It should create a public realm in which we can freely and robustly interact with each other.

* The rise of totalitarianism* is part of an overly managerial approach to politics that seeks to control everything we do, rather than liberate us to act on our own.

Core Question

The core question Hannah Arendt addresses in *The Human Condition* is: How can political action prevent the dangers of totalitarianism? Arendt realized that deep problems in society and politics had created the conditions in which totalitarian politics could take root. She believed the core problem was a failure to understand the importance of political action in creating a public realm that allows all people to participate. This public realm should be separated in some deep way from the concerns of managing the economy and social problems. In her view, this core problem manifests itself in the importance of the "social," or a focus on societal needs rather than political problems and the disagreements they produce. She wanted to deemphasize the social and reemphasize what she thought of as the political, feeling that the contemplative* political philosophers of her generation—philosophers who followed an abstract and theoretical approach—failed to understand that reflections on truth and beauty cannot address the dangers of totalitarianism.

To counter the dangers of Nazi* Germany, political action needed to be valued as a fundamental part of human life. Unlike the German political philosopher Karl Marx,* Arendt did not believe that the solution lay in creating new forms of economic distribution or new social rules. Rather, she believed people could resist creating new rules by focusing more on truly participatory political practices. Her originality lay in the distinction between the social and political. She argued that to prevent the rise of totalitarian politics, society needed to pay more attention to the political realm.

> *"... the emergence of the social realm, which is neither private nor public, strictly speaking, is a relatively new phenomenon whose origin coincided with the emergence of the modern age and which found its political form in the nation-state. In our understanding, the dividing line [between these realms] is entirely blurred, because we see the body of peoples and political communities in the image of a family whose everyday affairs have to be taken care of by a gigantic, nation-wide administration of housekeeping."*
>
> ——Hannah Arendt, *The Human Condition*

The Participants

Concerned about the managerial and controlling approach that pervaded politics, Arendt first examined its roots in the classical contemplative tradition embodied in the work of the foundational philosopher Plato.* Plato believed that only philosophers should govern. But Arendt preferred a more participatory approach to politics, noting: "The Platonic* separation of knowing and doing has remained at the root of all theories of domination."[1]

Arendt also argued against political and social scientists who believed that managing and controlling populations was the best way to prevent totalitarianism. In the United States, liberal* economists and political scientists such as John Kenneth Galbraith* and W. W. Rostow* argued that the only role politics needed to play was controlling the economy. Other contemporary political scientists such as Charles Merriam* and David Easton* argued that this managerial approach translated political life into statistics and mathematical models. The Austrian British philosopher Karl Popper,* a contemporary of Arendt's, made a similar point. In his 1945 work *The Open Society and Its Enemies*, Popper argued that theorists from Plato through Karl Marx had distrusted the practice of democracy. They did so, in his view, because they feared that democracy might arrive at the "wrong" answers. The British philosopher Bernard Crick's* influential 1959 book *The American Science of Politics* offered yet another view of the contemporary situation, criticizing the managerial and economics-focused study of politics. Arendt shared his concerns.

The Contemporary Debate

In contrast to her contemporaries, Arendt followed a unique line of thought. She sought to present a new form of politics that did not rely on managing society or economics. We may see this partly as a reaction to the rise of behavioralism,* which was just coming to the fore in political science, sociology, and economics; as its name implies, this approach to the study of social and political life focused on the analysis of individual behaviors. But as Arendt saw it, not all behaviors arise from the individual. Some actions, especially in the political realm, can arise unpredictably from communal desires. Revolutions and protest movements fall into this category. Other "actions" take the form of the institutions and structures that arise from those radical forms of politics. Behavioralism led analysts to focus more on statistics and management practices rather than on democracy, disagreement, and debate in political life. Arendt saw these behavioralist ideas as the heritage of the Platonic approach to politics. They disenfranchise people (deny them their rights) by allowing government to control their daily lives. Arendt also targeted Karl Marx, arguing that he focused his political theories solely on economic factors. Marx argued that we should interpret all political ideas and actions as arising from the economic structures created by capitalism.* Although Marxists and behavioralists represent very different ideological positions, both argued in favor of replacing the political sphere with the economic.

---

1. Hannah Arendt, *The Human Condition* (Chicago: University of Chicago Press, 1998), 225.

MODULE 4

THE AUTHOR'S CONTRIBUTION

KEY POINTS

* Arendt emphasizes the importance of action and appearance, which can only be found in the political realm.

* In *The Human Condition* Arendt lays the foundation for an active philosophy, which she also defines as a political way to philosophize.

* Arendt uses the experience of ancient Greek* democracy to construct a phenomenological* analysis of politics and to investigate *the human condition*—that is, an analysis that begins with subjective experience and consciousness.

Author's Aims

In *The Human Condition*, Hannah Arendt aimed to investigate conditions of both human existence and human activity. Some see philosophical reflection as the most important activity in human life, but she argued that political action remains most important of all: the act of coming together as a people to create institutions in a participatory and democratic manner. And how does she define "action"? In a particularly original way: "Action, the only activity that goes on directly between men without the intermediary of things or matter, corresponds to *the human condition* of plurality,* to the fact that men, not Man, inhabit the world. While all aspects of *the human condition* are somehow related to politics, this plurality is specifically the condition—not only the *conditio sine qua non** but the *conditio per quam** of all political life."[1]

In other words: plurality is both the cause and the engine of political life, and the most important things humans can do are to come together purposefully, to respect each other, and to try to create new institutions that exist for the good of all. These actions fundamentally define humans in a way that separates them from other animals. For Arendt, contemporary philosophy ignores this plurality, which she saw as the fundamental condition of human beings. Arendt defined plurality as the condition of living with and respecting the views and actions of others.

In *The Human Condition*, Arendt proposes a new approach to politics. Reacting against the abstract notion of humanity that reduces all people to the same type with the same interests and concerns, Arendt's approach accepts the world as it is: a place filled with many kinds of people with differing interests and concerns. For Arendt, politics is not just about governing or organizing economic and social relations. It is about living with others, acting with others, and creating something new.

> *"Arendt's* The Human Condition, *first published in 1958, offers a careful phenomenological account of the nature of human action, situating it in the public realm, drawing heavily on Aristotle and using an idealised model of the Greek city-state or* polis.*"*
> —— Dermot Moran, *Introduction to Phenomenology*

Approach

Arendt became the first scholar to address the contemporary

problems of totalitarianism* and democracy by analyzing the experience of democracy in ancient Greece over 2,000 years earlier. But she did not simply apply that model to contemporary politics. Instead, she used it as an inspiration for how we might encourage the creation of a new form of politics. By looking at modern politics through the history and ideas of the ancient world, she demonstrated the continuing relevance of the history of political thought. She also undertook a careful and critical analysis of the modern day. And she added a unique twist, moving away from the dry reflections of contemplative philosophy* to examine the potential of political action. No one else debating what modern democracy should look like took this approach.

The Human Condition's first chapter starts with a general explanation of the *vita activa** ("active life") and explores Arendt's general approach and aims. She identifies the different activities that constitute an active life—labor, work, and action. The next chapter focuses on the spaces (public and private) in which the three different human activities take place. The next three chapters examine these activities. She concludes with "The *Vita Activa* and the Modern Age," a chapter dedicated to analyzing the modern world using her theoretical framework.

Contribution in Context

The ideas developed in *The Human Condition* draw on a range of philosophical ideas and traditions, although Arendt's approach remained unique. The main theme—the *vita activa*—was directly inspired by the philosopher Aristotle's* concept of *bios politikos* ("political life") and the notion of *praxis** (roughly, "action") that he developed in his classic *Nichomachean Ethics*.[2] While classicists and historians of political thought dealt with Aristotle in the context of his own era, Arendt sought to make his ideas relevant to the modern day. She did this not by replicating all his ideas, but by using them to reorient political theory away from the search for truth and toward the search for successful democratic models. Arendt's encounters with phenomenology through her teachers Martin Heidegger* and Karl Jaspers* nourished her reflection about the idea of being in the world ("worldliness"), or the way human beings relate to the human world. Following Heidegger and Jaspers, Arendt focused on the description of the historical and existential* dimensions of the human experience (existentialism is a philosophical approach that emphasizes the lack of any governing order to the universe or reality). For her, "humanity should not be considered to have a permanent essential nature but only a certain condition."[3]

Arendt differentiated herself from Heidegger by inverting the traditional importance given to the *vita contemplativa** ("contemplative life") over the *vita activa*. She also criticized Heidegger's "neglect of cooperative human activity."[4] This exemplifies the originality of her approach. Heidegger believed that a philosopher should seek truth through reflection and avoid the messy world of practical politics. In Arendt's view, this allowed him to continue his pursuit of philosophy even as the world around him collapsed into war. In *The Human Condition*, she sought to reassert political activity as the most important activity in human life. She also wanted to create a practical work, looking toward the future. The keystone of her work lies in the distinction between the three activities—labor, work, and action.

---

1. Hannah Arendt, *The Human Condition* (Chicago: University of Chicago Press, 1998), 7.

2. Aristotle, *Nicomachean Ethics*, trans. Martin Ostwald (New York: Macmillan, 1962).

3. Dermot Moran, *Introduction to Phenomenology* (London & New York: Routledge, 2000), 306.

4. Moran, *Introduction to Phenomenology*, 288.

SECTION 2
IDEAS

MAIN IDEAS

KEY POINTS

* Labor, work, and action are the three activities fundamental to *the human condition*, action being the central political activity.
* Politics arises when human beings act among and with others and create something new.
* Based on the ancient Greek* experience of democracy, Arendt creates her own concepts to renew political thinking.

Key Themes

Hannah Arendt organized *The Human Condition* around the theme of the *vita activa*,* a Latin expression meaning "the active life." She identifies three types of active life: labor, work, and action.

Arendt believed that the history of philosophy had not dealt thoroughly enough with all three dimensions of *vita activa*. Instead of differentiating them, philosophers had merged them into a single entity. Arendt attempted to distinguish the three; and perhaps her most important contribution to political theory was in giving more attention to the third element—political action. Arendt attempted to restore a sense of dignity to political action. In her day, as in ours, people too often saw it as an arena in which politicians pursue their own interests rather than serve the public.

Arendt's focus on political action produced three important contributions to the study of politics. First, she moved it away from its fixation with formal rules and institutions. Instead, she focused on what political participants do. In this she differed significantly from behavioralist* social scientists, who were concerned with what might be analyzed through the observation of human action. Behavioralists also wanted to move the study of politics away from institutions such as law-making bodies, but they did so by reducing people to statistics rather than by trying to understand them.

Second, Arendt offered a full-scale critique of Marxism* and its focus on economics as the foundation for understanding politics; according to Marxist thought, history is driven by the struggle between social classes—a struggle in which economic interests play a particularly important role.

Finally, in her use of the ancient Greek model of politics, Arendt proposed an alternative to modern theories of democracy that were oriented toward consensus and compromise. Instead, she highlighted the conflict-based ("agonistic"*) dimension of democratic politics. For her, though, this did not require a turn toward violence. Instead, she envisioned a form of conflict that would continue to keep the political realm lively and contentious and should lead to the creation of new and productive forms of political life.

> "With the term vita activa, I propose to designate three fundamental human activities: labor, work, and action. They are fundamental because each corresponds to one of the basic conditions under which life on earth has been given to man."
> ——Hannah Arendt, *The Human Condition*

Exploring the Ideas

For Arendt, "labor" corresponds to people's biological life. Labor "assures not only individual survival, but the life of the species"[1] by providing for the biological needs of consumption and reproduction. Labor remains unceasing, as it creates nothing permanent. Arendt compares the laborer to the slave: given that the necessities of maintaining life dominate his existence, the laborer cannot be said to be free. Slavery here does not mean being owned by another, but being "owned" by the necessities of life. Those necessities prevent us from being able to see beyond the immediacy of our daily physical needs.

When Arendt speaks of "work," she refers to the fabrication of an artificial world of semi-permanent things not found in nature. A builder, an architect, a craftsman, or an artist provides "the human artifact,"[2] a common world of spaces and institutions in which human life takes place. Work differs from labor because it is not bound up with nature and survival. Human projects and creations transform nature, giving rise to objects and institutions recognized around the world. Thus, work carries with it a certain quality of freedom. But it follows an instrumental scheme: individuals are bound by the tasks set for them rather than being free to improvise and act as they wish.

"Action" corresponds to the activity that retains the greatest freedom from necessity. Means and ends come together in the action, which occurs in a public space of appearance, in which agents become visible. Activity appears in the plurality* of the public realm, among and with other people. For example:we may understand demonstrating in the streets as a political action because it makes a cause and principles visible. And it does so whether or not the activism succeeds. So for Arendt action and freedom are synonyms. Both represent the human capacity to create the new and unexpected, elements unconstrained by the rules of cause and effect.

Language and Expression

Arendt frequently refers to ancient Greek concepts, though she does not simply apply them to the contemporary context. She practices a two-step conceptual analysis: after situating the concepts in their historical and political contexts, she analyzes their transformations and meanings through the course of history.

Some readers may be confused by the absence of a systematic and single argument within the work. Fully understanding Arendt's unique, unorthodox, and complex thinking can require multiple readings. But *The Human Condition*'s plan follows the author's phenomenological* investigation. As a phenomenological theorist, Arendt approaches conceptual ideas by introducing their commonsense meaning, or what they "appear" to be. But she then alters them, presenting them as they *might* appear in other ways and to other people. She does not seek to develop a "true" definition of the terms under consideration. Instead she looks to create a set of categories that arise from the world of appearances. These categories evolve and develop as she uses them. She presents all the key concepts in the first chapter, and addresses them repeatedly throughout the book. It has been noted that Arendt developed her theoretical framework like an impressionist painter: as she emphasizes some core ideas, she exposes their characteristics with "small brush-strokes."[3]

---

1. Hannah Arendt, *The Human Condition* (Chicago: University of Chicago Press, 1998), 8.

2. Arendt, *The Human Condition*, 8.

3. Dermot Moran, *Introduction to Phenomenology* (London & New York: Routledge, 2000), 318.

MODULE 6
SECONDARY IDEAS

KEY POINTS

* Arendt formulated the idea of natality*—giving birth to new things through political action.

* Using her idea of political action, she highlighted how practicing forgiveness can reverse a political action, giving it a new political meaning.

* Our ability to act politically to create new realities offers us the potential to deal with environmental problems.

Other Ideas

In *The Human Condition*, Hannah Arendt introduces a secondary idea that she calls natality. She argues that natality gives action the ability to create something from nothing. Just as giving birth creates a new life, so political action creates something radically new—an institution, idea, or space that had not existed before. Of course, just as with birth, political action is just one part of a narrative. Other processes must precede it. But Arendt proposes that political actions can radically revise and create new things, just as a revolution may create a new social and political landscape, or a political institution might shape political life.

A second idea arising from her emphasis on political action is forgiveness. Critics have not always seen this as a political concept. But Arendt argues that forgiveness holds a unique place in political life because it reverses a previous action, situation, or condition. Unlike promising, an important form of political action that creates a bond between people, forgiveness radically disconnects individuals from their previous conditions and actions. It creates something new in the process, but only by destroying something that had existed before. Both forgiving and natality create new realities, but forgiving does so only by reversing a previous action.

"All three activities and their corresponding conditions are intimately connected with the most general condition of human existence: birth and death, natality and mortality."
—— Hannah Arendt, *The Human Condition*

Exploring the Ideas

At one level, Arendt's idea of natality remains a simple one. Giving birth is a fundamental part of human existence. Yet by making political action analogous with it, she breathes new life into the idea, giving it an important resonance it had lacked before. Natality, as a condition of political practice, celebrates the unpredictability of political action. Just as we cannot know how a child will develop, so we cannot know how our political actions will turn out.

This idea of natality also allows Arendt to link action and speech. Arendt argues that no action can take place without some narration to give it meaning. The narrative we construct around our actions reveals not only the action but the one acting. In political action, we create new spaces and ideas and we also recreate, give birth to ourselves. As Arendt puts it: "In acting and speaking, men show who they are, reveal actively their unique personal identities and thus make their appearance in the human world, while their physical identities appear without any activity of their own in the unique shape of the body and sound of the voice."[1] For Arendt, this means that when we narrate our actions, when we describe what we do in public, we create ourselves anew, giving birth over and over again to a new reality.

The other idea that Arendt draws from her conceptual apparatus is forgiveness. Arendt notes that the ancient Greeks,* to whom she turns so much, did not see forgiveness as a political virtue. Instead, she suggests that Jesus of Nazareth* made forgiveness a large part of political life. Arendt suggests that in making forgiveness so prominent, Jesus gave us the means to reverse political action, to sever us from our previous actions, but at the same time to create something new. "The freedom contained in Jesus' teachings of forgiveness is the freedom from vengeance, which encloses both doer and sufferer in the relentless automatism of the action process, which by itself need never come to an end."[2]

Overlooked

Arendt begins and ends her book with the relationship of humans to the earth. The introduction opens with a reflection on Sputnik,* the Soviet* satellite that was launched into space in 1957, only a year before the book's publication. Arendt noted that this represented the first time a man-made object had been moved into the arena of heavenly bodies. She felt it an important historical occasion. For Arendt, Sputnik's significance had less to do with the political circumstances that informed it than with the urge to leave Earth behind. She wondered whether this would be the first step toward the human race "escaping" the confines of the earth. She concluded by worrying about human alienation from the "world" or from the things, institutions, and spaces that give meaning to our lives. Few have explored Arendt's reflections on how our relationship to the world defines *the human condition*. Her point does not necessarily center on environmentalism, though it might have relevance for thinking about environmental issues. By emphasizing natality and political action, she clearly sees the potential for shaping the world in which we live, perhaps in radical ways, but she always keeps in mind how we are bound by our very human condition and this existence on Earth.

---

1. Hannah Arendt, *The Human Condition* (Chicago: University of Chicago Press, 1998), 179.

2. Arendt, *The Human Condition*, 241.

MODULE 7
ACHIEVEMENT

KEY POINTS

• Arendt's theory of action and politics successfully challenged the contemplative* philosophical approach and explained its incapacity to really understand *the human condition*.

• In the post-World War II* era, Arendt's account of action and politics as having the potential to create by acting together brought a message of hope.

• Many critics in the years after its publication underlined the book's lack of clarity and conceptual confusions.

Assessing the Argument

With *The Human Condition*, Hannah Arendt made an important effort to renew thinking around action and politics. Her emphasis on action influenced the development of contemporary political theory. She also intended to challenge the study of politics in the English-speaking world. She believed that political philosophers remained too concerned with Platonic* truths (the idea, drawn from the ancient Greek* philosopher Plato,* that "truth" can be found in the world of ideas), political scientists too concerned with formal institutions, and social scientists too concerned with reducing everything to economic forces. She focused on political action as a human practice in which a people creates and recreates itself. This put her in conflict with a range of different approaches, including idealist* philosophy (a tradition that focuses on the world of ideas as opposed to material reality), behavioralist* political science (a philosophy of social science that emphasizes the importance of analyzing human behavior, drawing heavily on statistical analysis), and Marxist*-inspired sociology and economics. Also, by using the ancient Greek philosophers to make her point, Arendt challenged assumptions built into modernity (a term used in history, philosophy, art, and politics to describe both a time period—the early twentieth century—and a general approach that focused on the importance of technology and scientific rationality when addressing social and political life).

Many scholars had begun to believe that the modern world defined by technology and progress had rendered historical studies of politics irrelevant. Critics continue to debate how successful Arendt was in reorienting the study of politics. Her work stood against so many different trends that few embraced it directly. Still, the challenge she raised remains important for the study of politics to this day.

"Hannah Arendt is preeminently the theorist of beginnings. All her books are tales of the unexpected (whether concerned with the novel horrors of totalitarianism or the new dawn of revolution), and reflections on the human capacity to start something new. When she published The Human Condition *in 1958, she herself sent something unexpected out to the world, and forty years later the book's originality is as striking as ever."*
——Margaret Canovan, introduction to *The Human Condition*

Achievement in Context

Arendt embedded *The Human Condition* in a historical conceptual framework. She intended to provide a new framework that could help people understand the modern world and some of the recent tragic events of the twentieth century. Arendt aimed her new science of politics at a wider audience than just academics. She wanted to provide an alternative to the dominant political context of her day—the tense nuclear standoff between the Soviet Union* and the Union States, and nations aligned to them, that defined the Cold War.*

More, she also undermined the American belief in technology and pragmatism as the solution to political problems, a belief associated with scholars such as American political scientists John Dewey and Louis Hartz. Arendt held an agonistic* democratic perspective (the idea that democracy should be founded on a kind of conflict beneficial to political life): politics is about acting in the public realm and seeking to promote ideas that not only provide radical alternatives but present the self in new ways. This did not sit well with the American pragmatist tradition, which emphasized solving problems by any means necessary. So neither side in the Cold War embraced Arendt's ideas.

Limitations

While influential in some contexts, the text's unique approach kept it from finding a wider audience. It can be difficult to translate the phenomenological* tradition, with its emphasis on appearance rather than some mystical "reality," into actual political analysis. Indeed, some have suggested that Arendt's idea of political action has no substance. People can "act," but the act itself rather than its outcome remains Arendt's greatest concern. So her ideas may seem unsuitable for studies of politics that seek concrete solutions to actual problems. In addition, her critique of Marx alienated many who draw from that tradition.[1] Even political theorists who might share some of her concerns have been critical of her work. The American political philosopher Sheldon Wolin,* for instance, argued that *The Human Condition* fails to theorize the social dimension of democratic politics adequately.[2]

Arendt did not fit well into any particular political orientation. As a recent German immigrant to the United States, she was just beginning to connect to the American context when she wrote *The Human Condition*. But she refused to attach herself to any particular political orientation, saying she was neither liberal nor conservative.[3] Because of this failure to align herself with a particular political ideology, her practical impact remained limited.

---

1. See Antonio Negri, *Insurgencies: Constituent Power and the Modern State*, translated by Maurizia Boscagli, foreword by Michael Hardt (Minneapolis: University of Minnesota Press, 2009).

2. Sheldon Wolin, "Hannah Arendt: Democracy and the Political," *Salmagundi* 60 (Spring–Summer 1983): 3–19.

3. Larry May and Jerome Kohn, eds., *Hannah Arendt: Twenty Years Later* (Boston: MIT Publications, 1996), 1.

MODULE 8
PLACE IN THE AUTHOR'S WORK

KEY POINTS

* *The Human Condition* remains Hannah Arendt's key theoretical work.

* It brought to fruition ideas that she developed in *The Origins of Totalitarianism* and which played out in later political essays and major works, such as *Eichmann in Jerusalem* and *On Revolution*.

* Arendt's unpublished works on a theory of politics also build on *The Human Condition*.

Positioning

In 1952, six years before she published *The Human Condition*, Hannah Arendt received a grant from the Guggenheim Foundation,* a philanthropic institution, to study Marxism* and totalitarianism.* This allowed her to continue themes she had developed in *The Origins of Totalitarianism* (1951), the work that first made her name as a scholar. In this work, she argues that totalitarianism arises from practices and projects, such as colonialism* (the unequal rule of one country by another), and anti-Semitism* (hatred of and discrimination against Jews), which both denigrate the equality of human beings. She also suggests that nationalism* (a political ideology in which defending the nation is the most important political principle), with its inherent exclusivity, also contributed to the rise of totalitarianism.

Pursuing this research led her to so many issues and questions that she never completed the initial project. But she did develop many ideas from it, such as reflections on the origins and conditions of the *vita activa** ("the active life"), which she presented in a series of lectures at Princeton University and the University of Chicago. These lectures, about the different human activities such as labor, work, and action, provided the basis for *The Human Condition*. Her later works deepened this exploration.

Arendt's works helped renew discussions on the nature of political life. "Within the space of four years, from 1958 to 1962, Hannah Arendt released three books, *The Human Condition*, *Between Past and Future*, and *On Revolution*, all of which had grown from the original Marxism book."[1] In essays compiled under the title *Between Past and Future* (1961), Arendt developed her ideas about political action in relation to authority, freedom, education, and history. And she elaborated on aspects of the theoretical framework she had put forward in *The Human Condition*, making the ideas more concrete. Her next book, *On Revolution* (1963), further developed these ideas in relation to the quintessential mode of political action—revolutionary politics.

> *"I set out to write a little study of Marx, but, but—as soon as one grasps Marx one realizes that one cannot deal with him without taking into account the whole tradition of political philosophy."*
>
> ——Hannah Arendt, in Elisabeth Young-Bruehl, *Hannah Arendt: For Love of the World*

Integration

We may see Arendt's body of work as an ambitious attempt to

build a new theory of politics. As she wrote to a friend in 1972, "we all have only one real thought in our lives, and everything we then do are elaborations or variations of one theme."[2] *The Human Condition* represented a pivotal point in her scholarly output, for it laid down the main theoretical elements of her work. She developed these themes in her studies of the philosophical approach of phenomenology.* She refined them as she explored the concrete manifestations of politics in her adopted country, the United States. And of course she continued to reflect on politics in relation to Germany and Israel throughout her career.

Arendt demonstrated her commitment to the practice of politics by pursuing an active political life. Two important controversies exemplify this. The first was her reporting for the *New Yorker* magazine on the trial of Adolph Eichmann,* a former Nazi* bureaucrat who had been kidnapped in Argentina by Israeli special operations forces in 1960. His trial—the first trial of World War II* crimes against humanity to be held in Israel rather than Germany—gained international attention. Eichmann was found guilty and was executed in 1962. Arendt attended the entire trial and published her reports both as magazine articles and eventually as a book, *Eichmann in Jerusalem*.

The book was controversial for two reasons. First, Arendt noted that Jewish agencies in various European countries helped facilitate the movement of Jews to the concentration camps,* making them complicit in the crimes. Jewish groups around the world argued that Arendt was blaming the victim, but in fact she was blaming the bureaucratic nature of political life. This became clearer in the phrase that she coined to describe Eichmann's actions: the "banality of evil." Some believed this detracted from the importance of Eichmann's crimes. But Arendt intended to point out that evil is not always committed in heroic, public ways; sometimes it occurs in secret, in the banal environment of a bureaucratic meeting. This corresponded to an argument she made in *The Human Condition*, which asserted political action as a way of revealing oneself, and castigated modern politics for hiding behind the veneer of bureaucracy.

The second public controversy in which Arendt became embroiled involved desegregation in the United States. Desegregation was the attempt to end the practice of segregation that relegated some individuals to a lesser or separate status, often along racial lines; in this case, the African American population. In 1957, nine black students tried to enroll at the Central High School in the city of Little Rock, Arkansas. But the state's governor blocked their entry. They were only allowed to enroll once the federal government had intervened. Photos of the teenagers being abused by whites objecting to desegregation drove Arendt to write an article for *Commentary* magazine in 1959, in which she criticized the children's parents for subjecting them to this abuse. Many read this as a defense of segregation. But Arendt based her argument on the distinction between the public and private realms—an argument she developed in *The Human Condition*. She believed that without a private realm, in which childhood and education take precedence, we cannot engage in the public realm of political controversy. For her, the Little Rock episode blurred the boundaries between the public and private.

Significance

The Human Condition arguably remains Hannah Arendt's most important book. It had a tremendous impact both inside and outside the academic community, and rewarded Arendt with international recognition. As her biographer, Elisabeth Young-Bruehl,* notes: "During the next twenty-four years, with her many essays and books, from *The Human Condition* to *The Life of the Mind,* Arendt won international fame and a place of pre-eminence among the theorists of her generation."[3] More importantly, *The Human Condition* remains a significant book in the development of Arendt's thought. The text offers an original contribution to philosophical approaches to politics; but we also need to see it in the broader context of her rich intellectual journey.

The theoretical and philosophical focus of *The Human Condition* meant that it did not expand Arendt's reputation far outside the scholarly realm. *The Origins of Totalitarianism* (1951) and *Eichmann in Jerusalem* (1963) won her greater acclaim, probably because they were more directly connected to the events of the day. Yet to understand those books we must first understand the theoretical arguments of *The Human Condition*, arguably her most significant theoretical work even though it may not be her most popular.

1. Elisabeth Young-Bruehl, *Hannah Arendt: For Love of the World* (New Haven: Yale University Press, 2004), 279.

2. Hannah Arendt, in *Hannah Arendt, For Love of the World* by Elisabeth Young-Bruehl (New Haven: Yale University Press, 2004), 327.

3. Young-Bruehl, *Hannah Arendt*, ix.

SECTION 3
IMPACT

THE FIRST RESPONSES

KEY POINTS

* Criticisms of *The Human Condition* focused on Arendt's use of other thinkers' work, her conceptual distinctions, and her account of "action."

* Arendt never modified her theoretical or methodological approaches in response to criticism. But she tried to explain her core ideas better in subsequent works.

* The various criticisms of Arendt's work reveal the different aspects of the intellectual, ideological, and political battlefields of that time.

Criticism

In the years following its 1958 publication, Hannah Arendt's *The Human Condition* attracted much attention and analysis. Critics focused on both the overall work and on specific elements of it. They pointed to three main areas: Arendt's methodological approach, the structure of her argument, and the way she used other thinkers' concepts.

Critics such as the American political philosopher Sheldon Wolin* attacked Arendt's methodology, in particular her references to ancient Greece.* In "Hannah Arendt: Democracy and the Political," he suggested the references to antiquity* were both anachronistic*—that is, they inappropriately projected modern expectations on to ancient times—and elitist.[1] He argued that Arendt failed to appreciate the complexity of Athenian politics, including the importance of the daily economic concerns that motivated some of the political debate.

The Russian British philosopher and political theorist Isaiah Berlin* criticized the text for lacking a structured argument. For him, Arendt "produces no arguments, no evidence of serious philosophical or historical thought. It is all a stream of metaphysical* free association. She moves from one sentence to another, without logical connection."[2] Crucially, the lack of a single overarching framework made her theory difficult for some to accept. She developed a plurality* of ideas in a complex and unorthodox argument inspired by many philosophers. Scholars often criticized her unique readings of other thinkers and her attempts to synthesize and incorporate their viewpoints into her own position.[3]

Third, the distinctions drawn by Arendt caused controversy. This stemmed primarily from the fact that she collected her concepts from different contexts. For instance, many feminist* theorists—thinkers engaged with the cultural analysis of the struggle for equality between the sexes—have criticized her separation of the "social question" from "political action." The German-born political theorist Hanna Pitkin*[4] confronted Arendt's distinction between private and public and the hierarchy that she placed them in, arguing that this tended to define motherhood and family as belonging to the private sphere and, therefore, lacking freedom. Marxists* also criticized Arendt's exclusion of economic and social issues from the political realm. They argued that doing so took questions of poverty and exploitation out of the political debate and made it impossible to address social injustice. Even some of Arendt's supporters considered this criticism significant.

> "While I feel that within the necessary limitations of a historical study and political analysis I made myself sufficiently clear on certain general perplexities which have come to light through the full development of totalitarianism, I also know that I failed to explain the particular method which I came to use, and to account for a rather unusual approach [to] the whole field of political and historical sciences as such. One of the difficulties of the book is that it does not belong to any school and hardly uses any of the officially recognized or officially controversial instruments."
> —— Hannah Arendt, "[Origins of Totalitarianism]: A Reply,"
> *The Review of Politics*

Responses

Arendt did not respond directly to criticism. But she did develop her thinking in ways that addressed some of her critics' concerns. In *On Revolution* (1963), she explained how an emphasis on the "social" can lead to further conflict and violence. She did this by comparing the American and French revolutions. In her analysis, the American Revolution* of 1775–81 succeeded because it focused on the political; the French Revolution* of 1789–93 failed because it arose from social concerns such as inequality (although the revolution created a democratic political system, it soon collapsed, leading to the rise of the dictator Napoleon Bonaparte in 1799).

In *Between Past and Future* (1968), Arendt demonstrated

how her insights could apply to more concrete situations, such as education and culture. *On Violence* (1970) proposed a radical new theory of power, which further developed the idea of political action already set out in The *Human Condition*. In this work Arendt argues that power does not mean being in a position to dominate others, which she sees as violence. Instead, it represents the coming together of many people to enact change. In the book, she uses this idea to examine the student protests against the Vietnam War* (a Cold War*-era conflict in which the United States engaged with North Vietnam between 1964 and 1973, with the loss of many lives on each side). While she supported these protests, she also criticized the way they sometimes focused on university governance rather than the war.

We may see Arendt's definition of power as a way to clarify the fact that political action does not simply mean a single hero acting alone. It can be a form of cooperative political action that might lead to new insights and institutions.

Conflict and Consensus

Interest in Arendt has recently increased, as scholars see her work extending into fields such as international relations[5] (the study of interactions between nation states). New efforts are underway to clarify her political concepts.[6] Her published works have been reissued and the Hannah Arendt Center at Bard College in the state of NewYork has given scholars access to her previously unpublished essays. This has resulted in new insights into her ideas.[7] Scholars currently agree that she played a crucial role in presenting alternatives to dominant modes of political analysis. Yet while her work has become more influential, we cannot say that political scientists or scholars have actually embraced it. Her unique approach to politics encourages readers to engage with her critically, rather than simply accept her ideas.

The *Human Condition* is, effectively, Arendt's attempt to conceptualize the implications of alienation from the world. If we must take action to renew the world, we must do so by connecting citizens back to one another and to an idea of a common world or a common life. Arendt felt the modern world had eroded this sense of commonality, and she was attempting to develop the theoretical foundation to restore it—so that, in turn, we can overcome the alienation of the world. This is why her idea of political action endures, more than half a century after she raised it.

---

1. Sheldon Wolin, "Hannah Arendt: Democracy and the Political," *Salmagundi* 60 (Spring–Summer 1983): 3–19.

2. Ramin Jahanbegloo, *Conversations with Isaiah Berlin* (London: Peter Alban, 1992), 82.

3. For an overview of various criticisms, see Walter Laqueur, "The Arendt Cult: Hannah Arendt as Political Commentator," *Journal of Contemporary History* 33, no. 4 (1998): 483–96.

4. Hanna Pitkin, "Justice: On Relating Private and Public," *Political Theory* 9, no. 3 (1981): 327–52.

5. Anthony F. Lang, Jr. and John WIliams, eds., *Hannah Arendt and International Relations: Reading Across the Lines* (New York: Palgrave, 2005).

6. Patrick Hayden, ed., *Hannah Arendt: Key Concepts* (New York: Routledge, 2014).

7. For instance, Hannah Arendt, *Responsibility and Judgment*, edited by Jerome Kohn (New York: Schocken Books, 2005); Hannah Arendt, *The Promise of Politics*, edited by Jerome Kohn (New York: Schocken Books, 2007); Hannah Arendt, *Essays in Understanding, 1930–1954* (New York: Schocken Books, 2005); and Hannah Arendt, *The Jewish Writings*, edited by Jerome Kohn (New York: Schocken Books, 2008).

MODULE 10
THE EVOLVING DEBATE

KEY POINTS

* The concept of natality* (the potential for political action to create new institutions and realities) can be usefully transferred to the creative arts.

* Although Arendt never founded a school of thought around her work, a large community of independent thinkers have used and discussed her theoretical framework.

* Many scholars from various disciplines have drawn on Arendt's work, most famously the German philosopher Jürgen Habermas.* This underlines the importance of her material.

Uses And Problems

The ideas Hannah Arendt explores in *The Human Condition* have been taken up in many different fields. The Scottish educator Morwenna Griffiths* has noted how Arendt's notion of natality can be useful in the arts.[1] Arendt's model of human affairs relies on change: every time new human beings come into the world and develop to the point of acting in it, the model changes. Arendt emphasizes natality over mortality in human experience, encouraging us to think of ourselves as beings who are first and foremost *born*. The fact of being born gives every human a unique life story that, in turn, makes each person unique. But Arendt develops this idea to suggest that we only acquire our unique life story to the extent that we *act* within the world, and disclose ourselves to the world and to others. All actions have consequences and we respond to those consequences by engaging in more actions.

This full sequence of actions and consequences comprises the story of any one person's life and creativity. The ability to be defined by the possibility of creating something new, to be constantly beginning rather than ending, has special significance for creative artists. Artists are, in a sense, fabricators with a capacity for originality. In Arendt's terms, they are actors requiring spectators—their action needs to take place in the public realm. In this way, action and artistry have a close connection to the condition of natality: the new beginning inherent in birth can make itself felt in the world only through the capacity for constantly creating something new.

> "Each time you write something you send it to the world and it becomes public, obviously everybody is free to do with it what he pleases, and this is as it should be."
>
> —— Hannah Arendt, "Remarks to the American Society of Christian Ethics"

Schools of Thought

Although Arendt's work developed a great following, she never tried to create a unified school of thought around her work during her lifetime. Two related but slightly divergent schools of thought have nevertheless formed around *The Human Condition*. The first approach, deliberative democratic theory,* has been spearheaded by the Turkish American political philosopher Selya

Benhabib[*2] and the German philosopher Jürgen Habermas.[3] Habermas used Arendt's distinction of *praxis** (action) versus *poiesis* (making) to differentiate the concept of work from what he calls "communicative action." For Habermas, "Hannah Arendt's principal philosophical work, *The Human Condition* (1958), serves to systematically renew the Aristotelian* concept of *praxis*."[4]

The second group of theorists who have used Arendt's work are agonistic* democrats (those who hold the position that democracy is founded on a degree of conflict), who include the feminist* theorist Bonnie Honig[5] and the political scientist Patchen Markell,[6] both Americans. Their works focus on the importance of creating spaces for politics, but they emphasize the conflicts inherent in the nature of political interactions. For them, disagreement remains a crucial part of democracy.

In Current Scholarship

The Human Condition has influenced many contemporary scholars. The two schools of democratic theories mentioned above may be the most prominent, but Arendt has also influenced other contemporary theorists from different disciplines. For instance, the idea of narrative as an important part of social and political theory influenced the work of the New Zealand-born anthropologist Michael D. Jackson.* Jackson used Arendt's work on storytelling to explore cross-cultural issues.[7]

In international relations, Arendt has been an important influence on contemporary scholars such as Patrick Hayden,* Anthony F. Lang Jr.,* Patricia Owens, and John Williams, scholars who draw on her work as a resource to counter the emphasis on global anarchy. In her works they find the potential for seeing global politics in new ways. In particular, Arendt's ideas have helped reinterpret debates about the use of force, war crimes, and global governance. Legal scholars have returned to her work, studying her ideas about legislation (law-making) and constitutional theory (theory about a nation's obligations and nature, as defined by law). These scholars have argued that she can be read as a theorist of law-making and not just of political action, especially in regard to narrating the political conditions that create the law.[8]

---

1. See Morwenna Griffiths, "Research and the Self," in *The Routledge Companion to Research in the Arts*, eds. Michael Biggs and Henrik Karlsson (Oxford: Routledge, 2011), 168.

2. Selya Benhabib, *The Reluctant Modernism of Hannah Arendt* (Thousand Oaks, CA: Sage Publishers, 1996) and Selya Benhabib, ed., *Politics in Dark Times: Encounters with Hannah Arendt* (New York: Cambridge University Press, 2010).

3. Jürgen Habermas, "Hannah Arendt's Communications Concept of Power," *Social Research* 44, No. 1 (Spring 1977): 5.

4. Habermas, "Hannah Arendt's Communications Concept of Power," 5.

5. Bonnie Honig, *Political Theory and the Displacement of Politics* (Ithaca, NY: Cornell University Press, 1993) and Bonnie Honig, ed., *Feminist Interpretations of Hannah Arendt* (University Park, PA: Penn State University Press, 1995).

6. Patchen Markell, "The Rule of the People: Arendt, *Arche*, and Democracy," *American Political Science Review* 100, No. 1 (2006): 1–14.

7. Michael D. Jackson, *The Politics of Storytelling: Violence, Transgression and Intersubjectivity* (Copenhagen: Museum Tuscalanum Press, 2002).

8. Christian Volk, *Arendtian Constitutionalism: Law, Politics and the Order of Freedom* (Oxford: Hart Publishers, 2015).

MODULE 11

IMPACT AND INFLUENCE TODAY

KEY POINTS

• *The Human Condition* explains why political protest continues to erupt and why such protests often fail to create new institutions.

• *The Human Condition*'s framework still challenges classical analysis by underlining the unpredictability of *the human condition*. Moreover, Arendt's conceptual distinctions question conventional ways of analyzing reality.

• Many discussions and criticisms—mainly about Arendt's theoretical distinctions—have enriched the ways in which scholars see the text in its original context.

Position

More than half a century after its publication, Hannah Arendt's *The Human Condition* continues to contribute to ongoing debates in political theory and political life. In 2000, a *Cambridge Companion* to Arendt—a volume discussing her ideas and work— was published, indicating the importance of her thought across a wide range of disciplines and approaches.[1] Her ideas have become influential in fields as diverse as international relations[2] and legal theory.[3] Throughout all these writings, the ideas introduced in *The Human Condition* remain central.

The basic question that Arendt asked in *The Human Condition* remains relevant to contemporary political debates. She challenges existing mind-sets by differentiating the social sphere from the political. On the basis of this distinction, she develops new ways of thinking about freedom and political action. Her ideas have great relevance in the current world order, especially as protests have erupted around the world in response to neoliberal* economic structures (economic structures in which government intervention in the markets is discouraged, and privatization encouraged). For instance, the worldwide Occupy Movements* (anti-capitalist action groups that have sprung up since the financial crisis of 2008) might well find Arendt's thinking helpful, being typical instances of political action. If these grassroots actions have failed to develop concrete alternatives, this might be because they focus excessively on the "social" rather than on the politics of creating new institutions.

> "Much as Arendt herself appropriated the political tradition of the West, not in the spirit of a scholastic exercise, but in the spirit of questioning and dialogue such as to orient the mind in the present, we too can engage with her work today to illuminate some of the deepest political perplexities of our times. One of these perplexities is the changing boundaries of the political in our societies, and with it the shifting line between the public and private realms."
>
> —— Seyla Benhabib, "Feminist Theory and Hannah Arendt's Concept of Public Space," *History of the Human Sciences*

Interaction

Arendt wrote about the way in which the rise of the social threatens the political. These ideas remain relevant today (when, for example, politicians inappropriately compare managing national debt to a family managing its household debt). But politics is much more than this. In Arendt's view, it should be about creating democratic spaces in which equality and freedom can flourish. Her theory of the social eating away at politics, which suggests a harsh criticism of consumer society, stands at odds with the theories of both liberal* and Marxist*-oriented scholars. Most political debate revolves around social policy, and tends to avoid explicitly political themes. Although British political parties, for example, continue to invoke the need for a constitutional convention (a meeting during which representatives of a people come together to draft a constitution) they have not convened one—perhaps because they remain more focused on pleasing constituencies with new policy initiatives than on facing the hard work of creating new institutions and ideas.

The Scottish Referendum* of 2014 (a vote taken on Scottish independence from the United Kingdom), one radical effort to confront the distinctly political question of sovereignty, generated much political dialogue in Scotland. The discussion suggested that Arendt had a point. People do not simply want social policies that deal with their daily lives; they want to engage in serious debate about political institutions and ideas. By insisting that the private and public, the social and political should be separated, Arendt remained unable to analyze the conflicts that arise when defining the boundaries between them. If this distinction between labor and action made her "unpopular with many on the left, her account of action brought a message of hope and encouragement to other radicals, including some in the Civil Rights movement* and behind the Iron Curtain"*4 ("the Civil Rights movement" refers to a number of related social movements in the US demanding equality for African Americans; "the Iron Curtain" was the name for the border between Eastern Europe and the West between 1945 and 1989).

The Continuing Debate

Many thinkers have criticized Arendt's private/public and social/ political distinctions for being too rigid. Feminist* scholars such as Hanna Pitkin* castigated *The Human Condition* for neglecting the issue of gender—a typical concern for feminist scholars, whose reading and analysis of culture focuses on the various implications of inequality between men and women. As the Turkish American philosopher Selya Benhabib* says: "For contemporary feminist theory Hannah Arendt's thought remains puzzling, challenging and, at times, infuriating."5 But Arendt's stance on gender remained more complicated than it first appeared. She defined labor as the activity dedicated to sustaining human life. Labor also provides for the biological needs of consumption and reproduction. These activities take place in the private realm of the household and are characterized by their necessity, so the person performing them lacks freedom. In this way, Arendt tacitly linked motherhood to notions of labor and, consequently, potential enslavement. Still, for her, natality* (birth) also represented new beginnings characteristic of freedom and political action.

Another example of critical discussion of Arendt's theory

comes from the sociologist Richard Sennett,* who also challenged her approach to labor. In *The Human Condition*, Arendt classified *animal laborans* (Latin for a laborer) as inferior to *homo faber* (Latin for worker/maker). In his book *The Craftsman*, Sennett criticizes this division of practical life, arguing that the craftsman's activity goes far beyond skilled manual labor.

1. Dana Villa, ed., *The Cambridge Companion to Hannah Arendt* (Cambridge: Cambridge University Press, 2000).

2. Anthony F. Lang, Jr. and John Williams, eds., *Hannah Arendt and International Relations: Reading Across the Lines* (London: Palgrave, 2006); Patricia Owens, *Between War and Politics: International Relations and the Thought of Hannah Arendt* (Oxford: Oxford University Press, 2008); and Patrick Hayden, *Political Evil in a Global Age: Hannah Arendt and International Theory* (London: Routledge, 2009).

3. Marco Goldini and Christopher McCorkindale, eds., *Hannah Arendt and the Law* (Oxford: Hart Publishing, 2012).

4. Margaret Canovan, introduction to *The Human Condition* by Hannah Arendt (Chicago: University of Chicago Press, 1998), xv.

5. Seyla Benhabib, "Feminist Theory and Hannah Arendt's Concept of Public Space," *History of the Human Sciences* 6 (1993): 97.

WHERE NEXT?

KEY POINTS

* *The Human Condition* gives us new insights into why political protests persist and what makes them successful.
* The originality and efficiency of Arendt's concepts allow many thinkers to use her theoretical framework in their own projects.
* With *The Human Condition*, Arendt elaborated a unique and unorthodox theoretical framework, which permanently challenged the ideas by which we analyze and understand our political world.

Potential

Today, what Hannah Arendt herself stood for is as important as the particular ideas set out in *The Human Condition*. She argued that "new beginnings cannot be ruled out even when society seems locked in stagnation or set on an inexorable course."[1] This emphasis on new beginnings has the potential to give meaning to protest movements. Indeed, it holds the key to their success. For Arendt, a protest movement represents the essence of political action—but it will fail if it focuses solely on "social" matters such as poverty or inequality. She understood that protest must begin with such matters, but she believed that, to achieve any concrete results, the protesters need to channel their energy into creating new institutions to address those problems. Arendt can offer insights into how we might create new political institutions to deal with the problems of our day.

Arendt's observations on the unpredictability of politics and her message of hope is likely to be developed further. For instance, her writings on Zionism*—the political movement to build a Jewish nation in the Middle East—of over half a century ago eerily describe the dangers that the world now faces. But she does not offer a simple call to action. For Arendt no human can take action for everybody; human beings in her perspective are plural. We live our lives as unique and very different individuals. Underlining the importance of creation, she states that hope comes from the continuous process of new people being born into this world, each capable of new initiatives.

> "As we stand at the threshold of a new millennium, the one safe prediction we can make is that, despite the continuation of processes already in motion, the open future will become an arena for countless human initiatives that are beyond our present imagination."
>
> —— Margaret Canovan, introduction to *The Human Condition*

Future Directions

Arendt's ideas may help us understand contemporary protest movements such as those that began in the Middle East in 2010 and have come to be called the Arab Spring,* or the Green Revolution* of 2009 following the controversial presidential elections in Iran. In these protests, people were reacting against the kind of rigid bureaucratic structures seen by Arendt as so detrimental to political life. In 2011, Egyptians created a new political system through their protests in Cairo's Tahrir Square. This new system focused only on order and practices of governance; it did not fundamentally change the Egyptian political system, so it failed. We may read this as reflecting Arendt's idea that political action can never be permanent, but must always be renewed. Her revolutionary understanding of political action makes personal projects subordinate to the more significant shared public realm. This both challenges and contributes to our understanding of contemporary politics. Arendt warns about "alienation from the earth"—namely, when "the human capacity to start new things calls all natural limits into question." She also cautions against "alienation from the world," when "automated societies engrossed by ever more efficient production and consumption encourage us to behave and think of ourselves simply as an animal species governed by natural laws."[2] Current scientific and social debates about DNA (the means by which genetic information is passed down the generations), atomic energy, and climate change demonstrate the timeliness of her concerns.

Summary

In her book on Arendt, Elisabeth Young-Bruehl states Arendt's principal question to be: "How shall we take political events, the political realm, seriously? The terms are simple, but the question is not."[3] A highly original work, *The Human Condition* renewed the debate about politics and philosophy with three key shifts of perspective: first, that action remains a fundamentally political activity of creation and freedom. Second, the corresponding understanding that action has potential power. And third, that there are conceptual distinctions between public and private, and between labor, work, and action. These three elements have changed the traditional analysis of politics, and imply an inversion of its scope. No longer limited to government or institutions, Arendt opens politics to the potential for action, for initiative in the public realm by unique human beings. For Arendt, general philosophical principles cannot regulate the political domain— and that itself raises philosophical questions. Her originality stands out in her fresh view of already familiar concepts. She transcends conventional analysis by proposing a unique and unorthodox approach that has permanently challenged the terms by which we analyze and understand our political world.

---

1. Margaret Canovan, introduction to *The Human Condition* by Hannah Arendt (Chicago: University of Chicago Press, 1998), xvii.
2. Canovan, introduction to *The Human Condition*, x–xi.
3. Elisabeth Young-Bruehl, *Hannah Arendt: For Love of the World* (New Haven: Yale University Press, 2004), 322.

1. **Agonism:** a term in political theory used to describe democracy that highlights disagreement and debate rather than consensus. This disagreement, however, is not violent and can actually benefit political life.

2. **American Revolution:** the revolution undertaken by American colonists in 1775 against the British government, which lasted until 1781, when the 13 American colonies created a single United States of America.

3. **Anachronistic:** a contemporary definition of a historical term or idea that fails to account for the differences between time periods. For example, it would be anachronistic to say that "democracy" is something that applied to ancient Athens in the same way that it does to contemporary Britain.

4. **Analytic Philosophy:** an approach to philosophy, largely found in Anglo-American universities, that focuses mainly on logic and meaning rather than metaphysical questions.

5. **Ancient Greece:** the period of Greek civilization that lasted from the eighth to the sixth centuries B.C.E.

6. **Antiquity:** generally used to refer to "classical" ancient civilizations prior to the Middle Ages, especially those of Greece and Rome.

7. **Anti-Semitism:** hostility, discrimination, prejudice, or hatred toward Jews.

8. **Arab Spring:** a term used to describe a series of violent and nonviolent protests, demonstrations, and civil wars that swept through the Arab world in 2010.

9. **Aristotelian:** philosophical approaches that draw on the ideas of the ancient Greek philosopher Aristotle (384 B.C.E.–322 B.C.E.)

10. **Behaviouralism:** a philosophy of social science that emphasizes the importance of analyzing human behavior rather than looking at formal institutions or ideas. Its methods draw heavily on statistical and quantitative analysis.

11. **Capitalism:** an economic system based on private ownership, private enterprise, and the maximization of profit.

12. **Civil disobedience:** an action, usually peaceful, taken to protest against a government, in which the protester accepts that he or she will be penalized by that government.

13. **Civil Rights movement:** refers to a number of related social movements in the US demanding equality for African Americans.

14. **Cold War:** a period of tension between the West and communist countries of the Eastern bloc, which lasted from the late 1940s (after World War II) to the start of the 1990s (with the fall of the Berlin Wall).

15. **Colonialism:** refers to the rule of one country by another, involving unequal power relations between the ruler (colonist) and ruled (colony), and the exploitation of the colonies' resources to strengthen the economy of the colonizers' home country.

16. **Concentration Camps/Death Camps:** camps created by the Nazi government in World War II that housed Jews, homosexuals, dissidents, and others deemed undesirable. Some camps were designed for work purposes, but most were designed for large-scale, mechanized slaughter of their inmates, usually in gas chambers.

17. *Conditio per quam*: a Latin phrase meaning "a condition that is sufficient."

18. *Conditio sine qua non*: a Latin phrase meaning "a condition that is absolutely necessary" (literally, a condition without which something cannot be).

19. **Contemplative philosophy:** a philosophical approach that emphasizes thought and reflection over action.

20. **Continental philosophy:** a school of philosophy found largely in France and Germany that draws on historical resources and seeks to explore broad metaphysical questions.

21. **Contingency:** the idea that we cannot predict the outcome of any course of action.

22. **Decolonization:** the process whereby nations gain independence from former colonial powers.

23. **Deliberative democratic theory:** the idea that deliberation (discussion) is an essential element of decision-making for a law to be truly democratic, and that voting alone is not enough.

24. **Empirical:** relating to something that can be verified by observation.

25. **Existentialism:** a philosophical approach that emphasizes the lack of any governing order to the universe or reality, associated with twentieth-century French philosophers such as Albert Camus and Jean-Paul Sartre.

26. **Feminism:** a school of thought based on analysis of society according to gender; it generally aims to institute equality for men and women in the spheres of culture, politics, and the economy.

27. **French Revolution:** a revolution undertaken by a wide range of groups in France, which began in 1789 and lasted until the execution of the French King Louis XVI in 1793. It created a radically egalitarian society for a period, until Napoleon Bonaparte came to power in 1804.

28. **Fundamentalist:** a term derived from nineteenth-century Christian theology to describe a belief system that seeks to return to the "fundamentals" or most important elements of a religious tradition. This usually means a literal reading of the religious text in question. It is now used to describe any believer who adopts a literal reading of their religious text and a conservative approach to their religion.

29. **Green Revolution:** the name for protests that followed presidential elections in Iran in 2009, against the reelection of the incumbent president Mahmoud Ahmadinejad.

30. **Guggenheim Foundation:** an American philanthropic foundation that funds research in the social sciences and humanities.

31. **Hegelian:** philosophical approaches that draw on the ideas of the philosopher

Georg H.W. Hegel (1770–1831). These approaches usually adopt Hegel's idealist philosophical approach and focus on how ideas determine our reality.

32. **Idealist:** in philosophy, a tradition that focuses on the world of ideas as opposed to material reality.

33. **Imperialist:** a term describing foreign policies that seek to create colonies or ensure the dominance of one state over many others. Imperialist can refer to formal empires, such as the Roman Empire, or more informal ones, such as that of the United States today.

34. **Iron Curtain:** the name commonly used to describe the border between Eastern Europe and the West between 1945 and 1989.

35. **Liberalism:** a current of thought that advocates the freedom of the individual and nonviolent change of political, social, or economic institutions.

36. **Liberal pluralism:** the belief in liberal political theory, and that a society should accept all forms of moral and religious belief, assuming that those beliefs do not harm others.

37. **Marxism:** a set of political and economic theories developed by the political philosopher Karl Marx and the social scientist Friedrich Engels in the mid-to-late nineteenth century. Marxist theory explains social change in terms of economics and also predicts a proletarian revolution to overthrow capitalism.

38. **Metaphysics:** in philosophy, metaphysics examines the way things are in the most fundamental way possible.

39. **Natality:** Hannah Arendt's term to describe the potential held by all political actions for creating new institutions and realities. This potential also leads to unexpected realities; just as no one can predict what a child will become, no one can predict what political actions will produce.

40. **Nationalism:** a political ideology in which defending the nation is the most important political principle. This reflects a belief that humans benefit from the culture, society, and politics of their particular nation more than from any

universal standards or international institutions.

41. **Nazism:** the ideology of the Nazi Party, which ruled Germany from 1933 to 1945. It is a variety of fascism that involves racism, anti-Semitism, nationalism, and national expansion.

42. **Neoliberalism:** a more recent version of liberalism (especially in the 1980s and 1990s), neoliberalism is a political position that advocates freedom of the individual and minimal government intervention in economic and social life.

43. **Objectivism:** in philosophy, a theory stating that reality exists freely or independently from human minds.

44. **Occupy Movements:** anti-capitalist action groups that have sprung up since the financial crisis of 2008.

45. **Phenomenology:** in philosophy, a philosophical study of the structures of subjective experience and consciousness. The German philosopher Edmund Husserl* (1859–1938) founded this school of thought.

46. **Platonic truth:** the idea drawn from the ancient Greek philosopher Plato that "truth" can be found in the world of ideas. Plato's theory is based on the notion that there are ideal forms of everything, which help us to define the objects, institutions, and practices of our real lives.

47. **Pluralism:** the idea that there are a multiplicity of ways of being in the world, all of which should be respected. This differs from tolerance, which assumes that we should simply accept other views. A pluralist approach claims we can benefit from these alternative views and ideas.

48. **Positivism:** in philosophy, a theory that confines itself to what can be known via empirical data, scientific methods, and objectivism.

49. *Praxis/poiesis:* *praxis* was the ancient Greek term for action. For Arendt, it represented the most important level of the active life. She used Aristotle's distinction between action (*praxis*) and fabrication, or making (*poiesis*) to underline the specifics of the concept of action in her theoretical framework.

50. **Resistance:** a term used to describe both violent and nonviolent forms of resistance to Nazi occupation, particularly in France during World War II.

51. **Scottish Referendum (2014):** a vote taken on Scotland's independence from the United Kingdom, in which the Scottish electorate voted to stay within the UK.

52. **Secular:** a term used to describe a political system or society that is not religious in any way.

53. **Social democrat:** A political position that combines liberal democracy with a socialist tendency toward redistribution of wealth.

54. **Soviet Union:** a union of socialist states on the Eurasian continent that existed between 1922 and 1991.

55. **Sputnik:** a Soviet satellite launched on October 4, 1957. It was the first satellite to orbit the earth.

56. **Totalitarianism:** a political system in which the centralized government holds total authority over society, controls private and public life, and requires complete subservience.

57. **Transcendental:** a term used to describe a reality that is beyond the observable or empirically verifiable. It is often used to describe religious experiences in which individuals feel a connection to the divine.

58. **Vietnam War (1961–75):** A conflict between the United States and North Vietnam in which the United States sought to protect its nominal ally, South Vietnam. It generated a great deal of opposition in the United States and is considered one of the few wars the US has lost.

59. ***Vita activa/vita contemplativa:*** *Vita activa* refers to a life dedicated to action. Its opposite is *vita contemplativa*, meaning a life dedicated to contemplation and thinking. For Arendt, *vita activa* corresponds more to the human condition, although thinkers have traditionally valued the contemplative life more highly.

60. **World War II (1939–45):** a global conflict fought between the Axis Powers (Germany, Italy, and Japan) and the victorious Allied Powers (the United Kingdom and its colonies, the Soviet Union, and the United States).

61. **Zionism:** a nationalist and political movement that sees the land of Israel as the rightful homeland of the Jewish people.

PEOPLE MENTIONED IN THE TEXT

1. **Aristotle (384 B.C.E.–322 B.C.E.)** was a Greek philosopher and a student of Plato. He is considered a founder of Western philosophy. His writings cover many subjects including physics, biology, logic, ethics, aesthetics, poetry, theater, music, and politics.

2. **Augustine of Hippo (354–430)** was a North African Christian theologian and philosopher. In his famous work *The City of God*, Augustine sought to reconcile the existence of the Roman Empire with Christian belief, emphasizing the importance of political order for spiritual life.

3. **Seyla Benhabib (b. 1950)** is a political philosopher at Yale University who specializes in Arendt and Habermas. She is known for combining critical and feminist theory. Her major work on Arendt is *The Reluctant Modernism of Hannah Arendt* (1996).

4. **Isaiah Berlin (1909–97)** taught at Oxford and was a philosopher, social and political theorist, essayist, and historian of ideas. He is known for his defense of liberalism, and his attacks on political extremism and intellectual fanaticism. His most famous work was *Two Concepts of Liberty* (1958).

5. **Heinrich Blücher (1899–1970)** was a German poet and philosopher. Blücher encouraged his wife Hannah Arendt to engage with the theories of Marxism.

6. **Margaret Canovan (b. 1939)** is an English political theorist who specializes in Hannah Arendt. She teaches political thought at the University of Keele. Her major work on Arendt is *Hannah Arendt: A Reinterpretation of Her Political Thought* (1994).

7. **Bernard Crick (1928–2008)** was a British political scientist. He was concerned with public ethics and politics.

8. **David Easton (1917–2014)** was a Canadian political scientist who spent most of his life teaching in the United States; he promoted behavioralism as the most important way to study politics.

9. **Adolf Eichmann (1906–62)** was a Nazi bureaucrat responsible for organizing transport of the Jews of Europe to concentration camps. After escaping to Argentina following the end of World War II, he was captured by the Israelis, put

on trial, and executed.

10. **John Kenneth Galbraith (1908–2006)** was a Canadian economist and diplomat. He was a staunch proponent of liberalism.

11. **Morwenna Griffiths (b. 1948)** is a professor of education at Edinburgh University who writes on philosophy and education.

12. **Jürgen Habermas (b. 1929)** is a highly influential German philosopher and sociologist. Over his lifetime he has made major contributions to studies of social and political theory, epistemology, and pragmatism. One of his main works is *The Theory of Communicative Action* (1981).

13. **Patrick Hayden (b. 1965)** is an international political theorist teaching at the University of St Andrews.

14. **Georg W. F. Hegel (1770–1831)** was a Prussian philosopher who argued that the world of ideas determines our reality. He introduced the idea of the dialectic, or the process by which opposing ideas interact to create our modern reality. He influenced the work of Karl Marx and many other philosophers.

15. **Martin Heidegger (1889–1976)** was an influential German philosopher who mainly worked on phenomenology and existentialism, exploring the question of being. Scholars consider Heidegger's *Being and Time*, originally published in 1927, one of the most important philosophical works of the twentieth century. He was romantically involved with Hannah Arendt until the rise of the Third Reich.

16. **Edmund Husserl (1859–1938)** played an important role in the foundation of the philosophical school of phenomenology, which looks at structures of the subjective experience and consciousness. His masterwork is *Logical Investigations* (1900–1).

17. **Michael D. Jackson (b. 1940)** is a New Zealand-born poet and anthropologist, and founder of existential anthropology. One of his major works is *The Politics of Storytelling* (2002).

18. **Karl Jaspers (1883–1969)** was a German philosopher whose work influenced modern theology, psychiatry, and philosophy. One of his major works is *Philosophy* (1932).

19. **Jesus of Nazareth (c. 4 B.C.E.–30 C.E.)** was a Jewish prophet who lived in Roman Palestine and was the founder of the Christian religion.

20. **Immanuel Kant (1724–1804)** was a German Enlightenment philosopher who aimed at uniting reason with experience; his major work is *Critique of Pure Reason* (1781).

21. **Anthony F. Lang, Jr. (b. 1968)** is an international political theorist who teaches at the University of St. Andrews.

22. **Karl Marx (1818–83)** was a German philosopher and revolutionary socialist. In his most significant work *The Communist Manifesto* (1848), written with Friedrich Engels, he developed the political and economic theories that came to be known as Marxism. Central to Marxist theory is an explanation of social change in terms of economics, along with a prediction that proletariat revolution will overthrow capitalism.

23. **Charles Merriam (1874–1953)** was an American political scientist who spent much of his career at the University of Chicago. He was a proponent of behavioralism and sought to promote pragmatic solutions to political problems in the US.

24. **Hanna Pitkin (b. 1931)** is a professor of political science at the University of California, Berkeley. She is known for her reflection on representation, *The Concept of Representation* (1967), and also *The Attack of the Blob: Hannah Arendt's Concept of the Social* (1998).

25. **Plato (c. 428/7 B.C.E.–348/7 B.C.E.)** was a classical Greek philosopher and founder of the Academy in Athens, who laid the foundations of Western philosophy along with Socrates and Aristotle.

26. **Karl Popper (1902–94)** was an Austrian British philosopher. He is one of the best-known philosophers of science of the twentieth century.

27. **John Rawls (1921–2002)** was an American moral and political philosopher. His *Theory of Justice* (1971) developed an approach that saw justice as fairness, answering to the demands of both freedom and equality of citizens in liberal democracies.

28. **W. W. Rostow (1916–2003)** was an American political theorist and economist. He was known for his conservative views, including his opposition to communism, and support of capitalism and theVietnam War.

29. **Richard Sennett (b. 1943)** is a sociologist at the London School of Economics and NewYork University who studies social ties in cities, and the effects of urban living on individuals. One of his main works is *The Craftsman* (2008).

30. **Ludwig Wittgenstein (1889–1951)** was an Austrian-born philosopher who worked mainly in England. His posthumously published masterwork *Philosophical Investigations* (1953) was collated and translated from German to English by his star student Elizabeth Anscombe. This work had an enormous influence on British twentieth-century philosophy.

31. **Sheldon Wolin (1922–2015)** was an American political theorist whose most famous book, *Politics and Vision*, argued for an approach to politics that avoids grand visions and focuses on democratic practices.

32. **Elisabeth Young-Bruehl (1946–2011)** was an American academic and psychotherapist who specialized in Arendt. Her most famous work on Arendt was *Hannah Arendt: For Love Of TheWorld* (2004).

 **WORKS CITED**

1. Arendt, Hannah. *Between Past and Future: Six Exercises in Political Thought.* New York: Viking, 1961.

2. *Correspondence with the Rockefeller Foundation.* Washington: Library of Congress, MSS Box, p.013872 (ix).

3. *Eichmann in Jerusalem: A Report on the Banality of Evil.* New York: Viking Press, 1963.

4. *The Human Condition.* Introduction by Margaret Canovan. Chicago: The University of Chicago Press, 1998.

5. *Life of the Mind.* Edited by Mary McCarthy. New York: Harcourt Brace Jovanovich (unfinished on her death), 1978.

6. *On Revolution.* New York: Viking Press, 1963.

7. *The Origins of Totalitarianism.* New York: Schocken Books, 2004.

8. *[The Origins of Totalitarianism]:* "A Reply." *The Review of Politics* 15, no. 1 (1953): 76–84.

9. *"Reflections on Little Rock."* Dissent 6, no. 1 (Winter 1959): 45–56.

10. Aristotle. *Nicomachean Ethics.* Translated by Martin Ostwald. New York: Macmillan, 1962.

11. Barber, Benjamin. *Strong Democracy: Participatory Politics for a New Age.* Berkeley: University of California Press, 1984.

12. Benhabib, Seyla. "Feminist Theory and Hannah Arendt's Concept of Public Space." *History of the Human Sciences* 6, no. 2 (1993): 97–114.

13. *The Reluctant Modernism of Hannah Arendt.* New York; Thousand Oaks: Sage, 1996.

14. Calhoun, Craig, and John McGowan, eds. *Hannah Arendt and the Meaning of Politics.* Minneapolis: University of Minnesota Press, 1997.

15. Canovan, Margaret. *Hannah Arendt: A Reinterpretation of Her Political Thought.* Cambridge: Cambridge University Press, 1994.

16. Griffiths, Morwenna. "Research and the Self." In *The Routledge Companion to Research in the Arts.* Edited by Michael Biggs and Henrik Karlsson, 167–185. Oxford: Routledge, 2011.

17. Habermas, Jürgen. "Hannah Arendt's Communications Concept of Power." Social Research 44, no. 1 (Spring 1977): 3–24.

18. *The Theory of Communicative Action, Volume 1: Reason and the Rationalization of Society.* Boston: Beacon Press, 1981.

19. *The Theory of Communicative Action, Volume 2: Lifeworld and System: The Critique of Functionalist Reason.* Boston: Beacon Press, 1981.

20. *The Structural Transformation of the Public Sphere: An Inquiry into a Category of Bourgeois Society.* Cambridge: Polity, 1989.

21. Heidegger, Martin. *Being and Time.* New York: Harper & Row, 1962.

22. Husserl, Edmund. *Logical Investigations.* London: Taylor & Francis, 1970.

23. Jackson, Michael D. *The Politics of Storytelling: Violence, Transgression, and Intersubjectivity.* Copenhagen: Museum Tusculanum Press, 2002.

24. Jahanbegloo, Ramin. *Conversations with Isaiah Berlin.* New York: Charles Scribner's & Sons, 1991.

25. Vlasta Jalušič, "Les éléments de la tradition en question. Hannah Arendt en ex-Yougoslavie et dans les États successeurs." Hannah Arendt abroad. Lectures du Monde. *Tumultes* 30 (2008): 81–108.

26. Jaspers, Karl. *Philosophy.* Chicago: The University of Chicago Press, 1969.

27. Kanellopoulos, Panagiotis. "Musical Improvisation as Action: An Arendtian Perspective." *Action, Criticism and Theory for Music Education* 6, no. 3 (2007): 97–126.

28. Kant, Immanuel. *Critique of Pure Reason.* London: Penguin, 2007.

29. Kawasaki, Osamu. "Hannah Arendt and Political Studies in Japan." In Japanese. *The Japanese Journal of Political Thought* 6 (2006): 82–109.

30. Leiter, Brian, and Michael Rosen, eds. *The Oxford Handbook of Continental Philosophy.* Oxford: Oxford University Press, 2007.

31. Moran, Dermot, *Introduction to Phenomenology.* London & New York: Routledge, 2000.

32. Plato. "The Simile of the Cave." Republic. Harmondsworth: Penguin, 1974.

33. Pitkin, Hanna. "Justice. On Relating Private and Public." *Political Theory* 9, no. 3(1981): 327–52.

34. Sandel, Michael. *Justice: What's the Right Thing to Do?* New York: Farrar, Straus and Giroux, 2010.

35. Schorske, Carl.E. "The New Rigorism in the Human Sciences, 1940–1960." *Daedelus* 126 (Winter 1997): 289–310.

36. Sennett, Richard. *The Craftsman.* New Haven: Yale University Press, 2008.

37. Smola, Julia. "La politique sans mots. Parler et agir en Argentine dans les années 1990." Hannah Arendt abroad. Lectures du Monde. *Tumultes* 30 (2008): 215–34.

38. Tassin, Etienne. *Le Trésor Perdu: Hannah Arendt, l'Intelligence de l'Action Politique.* Paris: Payot, 1999.

39. Young-Bruehl, Elisabeth. *Hannah Arendt: For Love of the World.* New Haven: Yale University Press, 2004.

原书作者简介

汉娜·阿伦特是 20 世纪最具影响力的思想家之一。1906 年，阿伦特出生于德国的一个犹太家庭，从小在无宗教信仰的环境中成长。但随着反犹主义的兴起，犹太人的身份成为了她身份认同的中心。1926 年，阿伦特在海德堡大学取得哲学博士学位；1933 年，阿伦特逃离德国。二战期间她在法国做短暂停留，后移民美国。她多数时间居住在纽约，在美国各大高校任教，并在世界各地进行演讲。1975 年，汉娜·阿伦特去世，享年 69 岁。

本书作者简介

萨哈尔·奥罗拉·赛义德尼尔：法国社会科学高等研究院社会学博士研究生。

安东尼·朗博士：圣·安德鲁斯大学国际关系学院院长，致力于研究政治理论中能动性、责任及惩罚的相关问题。

世界名著中的批判性思维

《世界思想宝库钥匙丛书》致力于深入浅出地阐释全世界著名思想家的观点，不论是谁、在何处都能了解到，从而推进批判性思维发展。

《世界思想宝库钥匙丛书》与世界顶尖大学的一流学者合作，为一系列学科中最有影响的著作推出新的分析文本，介绍其观点和影响。在这一不断扩展的系列中，每种选入的著作都代表了历经时间考验的思想典范。通过为这些著作提供必要背景、揭示原作者的学术渊源以及说明这些著作所产生的影响，本系列图书希望让读者以新视角看待这些划时代的经典之作。读者应学会思考、运用并挑战这些著作中的观点，而不是简单接受它们。

ABOUT THE AUTHOR OF THE ORIGINAL WORK

One of the twentieth century's most influential thinkers, **Hannah Arendt** was born in 1906 to Jewish parents in Germany. Her family did not raise her to be religious, but with the growth of anti-Semitism, Jewishness became more central to her identity. She received her PhD in philosophy from Heidelberg University in 1926 and left Germany in 1933. After a brief imprisonment in France during World War II, Arendt immigrated to the United States. Living primarily in New York city, she taught at universities across the country and lectured around the world. She died in 1975 at the age of 69.

ABOUT THE AUTHORS OF THE ANALYSIS

Sahar Aurore Saeidnia is a doctoral candidate in sociology at the Ecole des Hautes Etudes en Sciences Sociales, Paris.
Dr Anthony Lang is Head of the School of International Relations at the University of St Andrews. His work focuses on questions of agency, responsibility and punishment in political theory.

ABOUT MACAT
GREAT WORKS FOR CRITICAL THINKING

Macat is focused on making the ideas of the world's great thinkers accessible and comprehensible to everybody, everywhere, in ways that promote the development of enhanced critical thinking skills.

It works with leading academics from the world's top universities to produce new analyses that focus on the ideas and the impact of the most influential works ever written across a wide variety of academic disciplines. Each of the works that sit at the heart of its growing library is an enduring example of great thinking. But by setting them in context — and looking at the influences that shaped their authors, as well as the responses they provoked — Macat encourages readers to look at these classics and game-changers with fresh eyes. Readers learn to think, engage and challenge their ideas, rather than simply accepting them.

批判性思维与《人的境况》

主要批判性思维方法：阐释

次要批判性思维方法：创造性思维

汉娜·阿伦特的《人的境况》发表于 1958 年，这部作品是对"人之为人"的热切的哲学反思。

在讨论我们应该过怎样的生活、追求怎样的政治参与时，阿伦特的阐释能力引人注目，充分展现了批判性思维中阐释方法所能达到的最高水准。善于阐释的思想家，总是有能力厘清含义，质疑既有定义，提出更加合理、清晰的定义，并在此基础上使用其他批判性思维方法进行深入、广泛的论证。从各方面来看，《人的境况》就是一本关于定义的著作，阿伦特旨在提出以下观点：政治参与和积极参与社会生活是人类生活的最高目标。为此，她为"积极生活"划分了等级，将人类活动分为"劳动"、"工作"和"行动"，并根据三种人类活动参与世界的不同程度进行重新定义。通过对术语清晰、审慎的表述，最终将"行动"确定为人类生活的最高目标。

CRITICAL THINKING AND *THE HUMAN CONDITION*

• Primary critical thinking skill: INTERPRETATION
• Secondary critical thinking skill: CREATIVE THINKING

Hannah Arendt's 1958 work *The Human Condition* was an impassioned philosophical reconsideration of the goals of being human.

In its arguments about the kind of lives we should lead and the political engagement we should strive for, Arendt's interpretative skills come to the fore in a brilliant display of what high-level interpretation can achieve for critical thinking. Good interpretative thinkers are characterised by their ability to clarify meanings, question accepted definitions and posit good, clear definitions that allow their other critical thinking skills to take arguments deeper and further than most. In many ways, *The Human Condition* is all about definitions. Arendt's aim is to lay out an argument for political engagement and active participation in society as the highest goals of human life, and to this end she sets about defining a hierarchy of ways of living a "vita activa," or active life. The book sets about distinguishing between our different activities under the categories of "labor", "work", and "action"—each of which Arendt carefully redefines as a different level of active engagement with the world. Following her clear and careful setting out of each word's meaning, it becomes hard to deny her argument for the life of "action" as the highest human goal.

《世界思想宝库钥匙丛书》简介

《世界思想宝库钥匙丛书》致力于为一系列在各领域产生重大影响的人文社科类经典著作提供独特的学术探讨。每一本读物都不仅仅是原经典著作的内容摘要，而是介绍并深入研究原经典著作的学术渊源、主要观点和历史影响。这一丛书的目的是提供一套学习资料，以促进读者掌握批判性思维，从而更全面、深刻地去理解重要思想。

每一本读物分为 3 个部分：学术渊源、学术思想和学术影响，每个部分下有 4 个小节。这些章节旨在从各个方面研究原经典著作及其反响。

由于独特的体例，每一本读物不但易于阅读，而且另有一项优点：所有读物的编排体例相同，读者在进行某个知识层面的调查或研究时可交叉参阅多本该丛书中的相关读物，从而开启跨领域研究的路径。

为了方便阅读，每本读物最后还列出了术语表和人名表（在书中则以星号 * 标记），此外还有参考文献。

《世界思想宝库钥匙丛书》与剑桥大学合作，理清了批判性思维的要点，即如何通过 6 种技能来进行有效思考。其中 3 种技能让我们能够理解问题，另 3 种技能让我们有能力解决问题。这 6 种技能合称为"批判性思维 PACIER 模式"，它们是：

分析：了解如何建立一个观点；
评估：研究一个观点的优点和缺点；
阐释：对意义所产生的问题加以理解；
创造性思维：提出新的见解，发现新的联系；
解决问题：提出切实有效的解决办法；
理性化思维：创建有说服力的观点。

THE MACAT LIBRARY

The Macat Library is a series of unique academic explorations of seminal works in the humanities and social sciences — books and papers that have had a significant and widely recognised impact on their disciplines. It has been created to serve as much more than just a summary of what lies between the covers of a great book. It illuminates and explores the influences on, ideas of, and impact of that book. Our goal is to offer a learning resource that encourages critical thinking and fosters a better, deeper understanding of important ideas.

Each publication is divided into three Sections: Influences, Ideas, and Impact. Each Section has four Modules. These explore every important facet of the work, and the responses to it.

This Section-Module structure makes a Macat Library book easy to use, but it has another important feature. Because each Macat book is written to the same format, it is possible (and encouraged!) to cross-reference multiple Macat books along the same lines of inquiry or research. This allows the reader to open up interesting interdisciplinary pathways.

To further aid your reading, lists of glossary terms and people mentioned are included at the end of this book (these are indicated by an asterisk [*] throughout) — as well as a list of works cited.

Macat has worked with the University of Cambridge to identify the elements of critical thinking and understand the ways in which six different skills combine to enable effective thinking.

Three allow us to fully understand a problem; three more give us the tools to solve it. Together, these six skills make up the PACIER model of critical thinking. They are:

ANALYSIS — understanding how an argument is built
EVALUATION — exploring the strengths and weaknesses of an argument
INTERPRETATION — understanding issues of meaning
CREATIVE THINKING — coming up with new ideas and fresh connections
PROBLEM-SOLVING — producing strong solutions
REASONING — creating strong arguments

"《世界思想宝库钥匙丛书》提供了独一无二的跨学科学习和研究工具。它介绍那些革新了各自学科研究的经典著作，还邀请全世界一流专家和教育机构进行严谨的分析，为每位读者打开世界顶级教育的大门。"

—— 安德烈亚斯·施莱歇尔，
经济合作与发展组织教育与技能司司长

"《世界思想宝库钥匙丛书》直面大学教育的巨大挑战……他们组建了一支精干而活跃的学者队伍，来推出在研究广度上颇具新意的教学材料。"

—— 布罗尔斯教授、勋爵，剑桥大学前校长

"《世界思想宝库钥匙丛书》的愿景令人赞叹。它通过分析和阐释那些曾深刻影响人类思想以及社会、经济发展的经典文本，提供了新的学习方法。它推动批判性思维，这对于任何社会和经济体来说都是至关重要的。这就是未来的学习方法。"

—— 查尔斯·克拉克阁下，英国前教育大臣

"对于那些影响了各自领域的著作，《世界思想宝库钥匙丛书》能让人们立即了解到围绕那些著作展开的评论性言论，这让该系列图书成为在这些领域从事研究的师生们不可或缺的资源。"

—— 威廉·特朗佐教授，加利福尼亚大学圣地亚哥分校

"Macat offers an amazing first-of-its-kind tool for interdisciplinary learning and research. Its focus on works that transformed their disciplines and its rigorous approach, drawing on the world's leading experts and educational institutions, opens up a world-class education to anyone."

—— Andreas Schleicher, Director for Education and Skills, Organisation for Economic Co-operation and Development

"Macat is taking on some of the major challenges in university education... They have drawn together a strong team of active academics who are producing teaching materials that are novel in the breadth of their approach."

—— Prof Lord Broers, former Vice-Chancellor of the University of Cambridge

"The Macat vision is exceptionally exciting. It focuses upon new modes of learning which analyse and explain seminal texts which have profoundly influenced world thinking and so social and economic development. It promotes the kind of critical thinking which is essential for any society and economy. This is the learning of the future."

—— Rt Hon Charles Clarke, former UK Secretary of State for Education

"The Macat analyses provide immediate access to the critical conversation surrounding the books that have shaped their respective discipline, which will make them an invaluable resource to all of those, students and teachers, working in the field."

—— Prof William Tronzo, University of California at San Diego

TITLE	中文书名	类别
An Analysis of Arjun Appadurai's *Modernity at Large: Cultural Dimensions of Globalization*	解析阿尔君·阿帕杜莱《消失的现代性：全球化的文化维度》	人类学
An Analysis of Claude Lévi-Strauss's *Structural Anthropology*	解析克劳德-列维-施特劳斯《结构人类学》	人类学
An Analysis of Marcel Mauss's *The Gift*	解析马塞尔·莫斯《礼物》	人类学
An Analysis of Jared M. Diamond's *Guns, Germs, and Steel: The Fate of Human Societies*	解析贾雷德·戴蒙德《枪炮、病菌与钢铁：人类社会的命运》	人类学
An Analysis of Clifford Geertz's *The Interpretation of Cultures*	解析克利福德·格尔茨《文化的解释》	人类学
An Analysis of Philippe Ariès's *Centuries of Childhood: A Social History of Family Life*	解析菲力浦·阿利埃斯《儿童的世纪：旧制度下的儿童和家庭生活》	人类学
An Analysis of W. Chan Kim & Renée Mauborgne's *Blue Ocean Strategy*	解析金伟灿/勒妮·莫博涅《蓝海战略》	商业
An Analysis of John P. Kotter's *Leading Change*	解析约翰·P. 科特《领导变革》	商业
An Analysis of Michael E. Porter's *Competitive Strategy: Techniques for Analyzing Industries and Competitors*	解析迈克尔·E. 波特《竞争战略：分析产业和竞争对手的技术》	商业
An Analysis of Jean Lave & Etienne Wenger's *Situated Learning: Legitimate Peripheral Participation*	解析琼·莱夫/艾蒂纳·温格《情境学习：合法的边缘性参与》	商业
An Analysis of Douglas McGregor's *The Human Side of Enterprise*	解析道格拉斯·麦格雷戈《企业的人性面》	商业
An Analysis of Milton Friedman's *Capitalism and Freedom*	解析米尔顿·弗里德曼《资本主义与自由》	商业
An Analysis of Ludwig von Mises's *The Theory of Money and Credit*	解析路德维希·冯·米塞斯《货币和信用理论》	经济学
An Analysis of Adam Smith's *The Wealth of Nations*	解析亚当·斯密《国富论》	经济学
An Analysis of Thomas Piketty's *Capital in the Twenty-First Century*	解析托马斯·皮凯蒂《21世纪资本论》	经济学
An Analysis of Nassim Nicholas Taleb's *The Black Swan: The Impact of the Highly Improbable*	解析纳西姆·尼古拉斯·塔勒布《黑天鹅：如何应对不可预知的未来》	经济学
An Analysis of Ha-Joon Chang's *Kicking Away the Ladder*	解析张夏准《富国陷阱：发达国家为何踢开梯子》	经济学
An Analysis of Thomas Robert Malthus's *An Essay on the Principle of Population*	解析托马斯·罗伯特·马尔萨斯《人口论》	经济学

An Analysis of John Maynard Keynes's *The General Theory of Employment, Interest and Money*	解析约翰·梅纳德·凯恩斯《就业、利息和货币通论》	经济学
An Analysis of Milton Friedman's *The Role of Monetary Policy*	解析米尔顿·弗里德曼《货币政策的作用》	经济学
An Analysis of Burton G. Malkiel's *A Random Walk Down Wall Street*	解析伯顿·G.马尔基尔《漫步华尔街》	经济学
An Analysis of Friedrich A. Hayek's *The Road to Serfdom*	解析弗里德里希·A.哈耶克《通往奴役之路》	经济学
An Analysis of Charles P. Kindleberger's *Manias, Panics, and Crashes: A History of Financial Crises*	解析查尔斯·P.金德尔伯格《疯狂、惊恐和崩溃：金融危机史》	经济学
An Analysis of Amartya Sen's *Development as Freedom*	解析阿马蒂亚·森《以自由看待发展》	经济学
An Analysis of Rachel Carson's *Silent Spring*	解析蕾切尔·卡森《寂静的春天》	地理学
An Analysis of Charles Darwin's *On the Origin of Species: by Means of Natural Selection, or The Preservation of Favoured Races in the Struggle for Life*	解析查尔斯·达尔文《物种起源》	地理学
An Analysis of World Commission on Environment and Development's *The Brundtland Report, Our Common Future*	解析世界环境与发展委员会《布伦特兰报告：我们共同的未来》	地理学
An Analysis of James E. Lovelock's *Gaia: A New Look at Life on Earth*	解析詹姆斯·E.拉伍洛克《盖娅：地球生命的新视野》	地理学
An Analysis of Paul Kennedy's *The Rise and Fall of the Great Powers: Economic Change and Military Conflict from 1500—2000*	解析保罗·肯尼迪《大国的兴衰：1500—2000年的经济变革与军事冲突》	历史
An Analysis of Janet L. Abu-Lughod's *Before European Hegemony: The World System A. D. 1250—1350*	解析珍妮特·L.阿布-卢格霍德《欧洲霸权之前：1250—1350年的世界体系》	历史
An Analysis of Alfred W. Crosby's *The Columbian Exchange: Biological and Cultural Consequences of 1492*	解析艾尔弗雷德·W.克罗斯比《哥伦布大交换：1492年以后的生物影响和文化冲击》	历史
An Analysis of Tony Judt's *Postwar: A History of Europe since 1945*	解析托尼·朱特《战后欧洲史》	历史
An Analysis of Richard J. Evans's *In Defence of History*	解析理查德·J.艾文斯《捍卫历史》	历史
An Analysis of Eric Hobsbawm's *The Age of Revolution: Europe 1789–1848*	解析艾瑞克·霍布斯鲍姆《革命的年代：欧洲1789—1848年》	历史

An Analysis of Roland Barthes's *Mythologies*	解析罗兰·巴特《神话学》	文学与批判理论
An Analysis of Simon de Beauvoir's *The Second Sex*	解析西蒙娜·德·波伏娃《第二性》	文学与批判理论
An Analysis of Edward W. Said's *Orientalism*	解析爱德华·W. 萨义德《东方主义》	文学与批判理论
An Analysis of Virginia Woolf's *A Room of One's Own*	解析弗吉尼亚·伍尔芙《一间自己的房间》	文学与批判理论
An Analysis of Judith Butler's *Gender Trouble*	解析朱迪斯·巴特勒《性别麻烦》	文学与批判理论
An Analysis of Ferdinand de Saussure's *Course in General Linguistics*	解析费尔迪南·德·索绪尔《普通语言学教程》	文学与批判理论
An Analysis of Susan Sontag's *On Photography*	解析苏珊·桑塔格《论摄影》	文学与批判理论
An Analysis of Walter Benjamin's *The Work of Art in the Age of Mechanical Reproduction*	解析瓦尔特·本雅明《机械复制时代的艺术作品》	文学与批判理论
An Analysis of W.E.B. Du Bois's *The Souls of Black Folk*	解析 W.E.B. 杜波依斯《黑人的灵魂》	文学与批判理论
An Analysis of Plato's *The Republic*	解析柏拉图《理想国》	哲学
An Analysis of Plato's *Symposium*	解析柏拉图《会饮篇》	哲学
An Analysis of Aristotle's *Metaphysics*	解析亚里士多德《形而上学》	哲学
An Analysis of Aristotle's *Nicomachean Ethics*	解析亚里士多德《尼各马可伦理学》	哲学
An Analysis of Immanuel Kant's *Critique of Pure Reason*	解析伊曼努尔·康德《纯粹理性批判》	哲学
An Analysis of Ludwig Wittgenstein's *Philosophical Investigations*	解析路德维希·维特根斯坦《哲学研究》	哲学
An Analysis of G.W.F. Hegel's *Phenomenology of Spirit*	解析 G.W.F. 黑格尔《精神现象学》	哲学
An Analysis of Baruch Spinoza's *Ethics*	解析巴鲁赫·斯宾诺莎《伦理学》	哲学
An Analysis of Hannah Arendt's *The Human Condition*	解析汉娜·阿伦特《人的境况》	哲学
An Analysis of G.E.M. Anscombe's *Modern Moral Philosophy*	解析 G.E.M. 安斯康姆《现代道德哲学》	哲学
An Analysis of David Hume's *An Enquiry Concerning Human Understanding*	解析大卫·休谟《人类理解研究》	哲学

An Analysis of Søren Kierkegaard's *Fear and Trembling*	解析索伦·克尔凯郭尔《恐惧与战栗》	哲学
An Analysis of René Descartes's *Meditations on First Philosophy*	解析勒内·笛卡尔《第一哲学沉思录》	哲学
An Analysis of Friedrich Nietzsche's *On the Genealogy of Morality*	解析弗里德里希·尼采《论道德的谱系》	哲学
An Analysis of Gilbert Ryle's *The Concept of Mind*	解析吉尔伯特·赖尔《心的概念》	哲学
An Analysis of Thomas Kuhn's *The Structure of Scientific Revolutions*	解析托马斯·库恩《科学革命的结构》	哲学
An Analysis of John Stuart Mill's *Utilitarianism*	解析约翰·斯图亚特·穆勒《功利主义》	哲学
An Analysis of Aristotle's *Politics*	解析亚里士多德《政治学》	政治学
An Analysis of Niccolò Machiavelli's *The Prince*	解析尼科洛·马基雅维利《君主论》	政治学
An Analysis of Karl Marx's *Capital*	解析卡尔·马克思《资本论》	政治学
An Analysis of Benedict Anderson's *Imagined Communities*	解析本尼迪克特·安德森《想象的共同体》	政治学
An Analysis of Samuel P. Huntington's *The Clash of Civilizations and the Remaking of World Order*	解析塞缪尔·P.亨廷顿《文明的冲突与世界秩序的重建》	政治学
An Analysis of Alexis de Tocqueville's *Democracy in America*	解析阿列克西·德·托克维尔《论美国的民主》	政治学
An Analysis of John A. Hobson's *Imperialism: A Study*	解析约翰·A.霍布森《帝国主义》	政治学
An Analysis of Thomas Paine's *Common Sense*	解析托马斯·潘恩《常识》	政治学
An Analysis of John Rawls's *A Theory of Justice*	解析约翰·罗尔斯《正义论》	政治学
An Analysis of Francis Fukuyama's *The End of History and the Last Man*	解析弗朗西斯·福山《历史的终结与最后的人》	政治学
An Analysis of John Locke's *Two Treatises of Government*	解析约翰·洛克《政府论》	政治学
An Analysis of Sun Tzu's *The Art of War*	解析孙武《孙子兵法》	政治学
An Analysis of Henry Kissinger's *World Order: Reflections on the Character of Nations and the Course of History*	解析亨利·基辛格《世界秩序》	政治学
An Analysis of Jean-Jacques Rousseau's *The Social Contract*	解析让-雅克·卢梭《社会契约论》	政治学

An Analysis of Odd Arne Westad's *The Global Cold War: Third World Interventions and the Making of Our Times*	解析文安立《全球冷战：美苏对第三世界的干涉与当代世界的形成》	政治学
An Analysis of Sigmund Freud's *The Interpretation of Dreams*	解析西格蒙德·弗洛伊德《梦的解析》	心理学
An Analysis of William James' *The Principles of Psychology*	解析威廉·詹姆斯《心理学原理》	心理学
An Analysis of Philip Zimbardo's *The Lucifer Effect*	解析菲利普·津巴多《路西法效应》	心理学
An Analysis of Leon Festinger's *A Theory of Cognitive Dissonance*	解析利昂·费斯汀格《认知失调论》	心理学
An Analysis of Richard H. Thaler & Cass R. Sunstein's *Nudge: Improving Decisions about Health, Wealth, and Happiness*	解析理查德·H.泰勒/卡斯·R.桑斯坦《助推：如何做出有关健康、财富和幸福的更优决策》	心理学
An Analysis of Gordon Allport's *The Nature of Prejudice*	解析高尔登·奥尔波特《偏见的本质》	心理学
An Analysis of Steven Pinker's *The Better Angels of Our Nature: Why Violence Has Declined*	解析斯蒂芬·平克《人性中的善良天使：暴力为什么会减少》	心理学
An Analysis of Stanley Milgram's *Obedience to Authority*	解析斯坦利·米尔格拉姆《对权威的服从》	心理学
An Analysis of Betty Friedan's *The Feminine Mystique*	解析贝蒂·弗里丹《女性的奥秘》	心理学
An Analysis of David Riesman's *The Lonely Crowd: A Study of the Changing American Character*	解析大卫·理斯曼《孤独的人群：美国人社会性格演变之研究》	社会学
An Analysis of Franz Boas's *Race, Language and Culture*	解析弗朗兹·博厄斯《种族、语言与文化》	社会学
An Analysis of Pierre Bourdieu's *Outline of a Theory of Practice*	解析皮埃尔·布尔迪厄《实践理论大纲》	社会学
An Analysis of Max Weber's *The Protestant Ethic and the Spirit of Capitalism*	解析马克斯·韦伯《新教伦理与资本主义精神》	社会学
An Analysis of Jane Jacobs's *The Death and Life of Great American Cities*	解析简·雅各布斯《美国大城市的死与生》	社会学
An Analysis of C. Wright Mills's *The Sociological Imagination*	解析C.赖特·米尔斯《社会学的想象力》	社会学
An Analysis of Robert E. Lucas Jr.'s *Why Doesn't Capital Flow from Rich to Poor Countries?*	解析小罗伯特·E.卢卡斯《为何资本不从富国流向穷国？》	社会学

An Analysis of Émile Durkheim's *On Suicide*	解析埃米尔·迪尔凯姆《自杀论》	社会学
An Analysis of Eric Hoffer's *The True Believer: Thoughts on the Nature of Mass Movements*	解析埃里克·霍弗《狂热分子：群众运动圣经》	社会学
An Analysis of Jared M. Diamond's *Collapse: How Societies Choose to Fail or Survive*	解析贾雷德·M.戴蒙德《大崩溃：社会如何选择兴亡》	社会学
An Analysis of Michel Foucault's *The History of Sexuality Vol. 1: The Will to Knowledge*	解析米歇尔·福柯《性史（第一卷）：求知意志》	社会学
An Analysis of Michel Foucault's *Discipline and Punish*	解析米歇尔·福柯《规训与惩罚》	社会学
An Analysis of Richard Dawkins's *The Selfish Gene*	解析理查德·道金斯《自私的基因》	社会学
An Analysis of Antonio Gramsci's *Prison Notebooks*	解析安东尼奥·葛兰西《狱中札记》	社会学
An Analysis of Augustine's *Confessions*	解析奥古斯丁《忏悔录》	神学
An Analysis of C. S. Lewis's *The Abolition of Man*	解析 C. S. 路易斯《人之废》	神学

图书在版编目（CIP）数据

解析汉娜·阿伦特《人的境况》：汉、英 / 萨哈尔·奥罗拉·赛义德尼尔
（Sahar Aurore Saeidnia），安东尼·朗（Anthony Lang）著；
刘雨桐译 . —上海：上海外语教育出版社，2019
（世界思想宝库钥匙丛书）
ISBN 978-7-5446-6028-0

Ⅰ. ①解… Ⅱ. ①萨… ②安… ③刘… Ⅲ. ①人学－研究 Ⅳ. ①C912.1

中国版本图书馆CIP数据核字（2019）第232120号

This Chinese-English bilingual edition of *An Analysis of Hannah Arendt's* The Human Condition
is published by arrangement with Macat International Limited.
Licensed for sale throughout the world.

本书汉英双语版由Macat国际有限公司授权上海外语教育出版社有限公司出版。
供在全世界范围内发行、销售。

图字：09 – 2018 – 549

出版发行：上海外语教育出版社
（上海外国语大学内） 邮编：200083
电　　话： 021-65425300（总机）
电子邮箱： bookinfo@sflep.com.cn
网　　址： http://www.sflep.com
责任编辑： 梁瀚杰

印　　刷：上海华教印务有限公司
开　　本： 890×1240　1/32　印张 5.5　字数 112千字
版　　次： 2020 年 5 月第 1 版　　2020 年 5 月第 1 次印刷
印　　数： 2 100 册

书　　号： ISBN 978-7-5446-6028-0
定　　价： 30.00 元
本版图书如有印装质量问题, 可向本社调换
质量服务热线：4008-213-263　电子邮箱：**editorial@sflep.com**